THE MURDERS THAT WAS THE

Nobody wanted to think that an attractive, seemingly loving mother like Diana Lumbrera would callously kill her infant children one after another in a spree of slaying that went on year after year, birth after birth.

The doctors who certified the deaths as "natural" didn't want to believe it, even as the macabre death toll mounted.

The authorities who refused to investigate the carnage didn't want to believe it, despite the lengthening list of little corpses.

Until the day that little José Lumbrera was brought dead to a Kansas hospital. . . . And this time a doctor refused to look the other way. . . . Two cops followed leads that revealed a scope of savagery beyond their wildest suspicions. . . . A prosecutor put his career and faith in the law on the line as he faced a brilliant defense attorney who pulled out all the legal stops. . . . And a jury was faced with evidence that seemed so evil, it was incredible. . . .

MOMMY'S LITTLE ANGELS

The True Story of a Mother Who Murdered Seven Children

MOMMY'S LITTLE ANGELS

The True Story of a Mother Who Murdered Seven Children

Mary Lou Cavenaugh

AN ONYX BOOK

ONYX
Published by the Penguin Group
Penguin Books USA Inc., 375 Hudson Street,
New York, New York 10014, U.S.A.
Penguin Books Ltd, 27 Wrights Lane,
London W8 5TZ, England
Penguin Books Australia Ltd, Ringwood,
Victoria, Australia
Penguin Books Canada Ltd, 10 Alcorn Avenue,
Toronto, Ontario, Canada M4V 3B2
Penguin Books (N.Z.) Ltd, 182–190 Wairau Road,
Auckland 10, New Zealand

Penguin Books Ltd, Registered Offices:
Harmondsworth, Middlesex, England

First published by Onyx, an imprint of Dutton Signet,
a division of Penguin Books USA Inc.

First Printing, June, 1995
10 9 8 7 6 5 4 3 2 1

 REGISTERED TRADEMARK—MARCA REGISTRADA

Printed in the United States of America

For my beautiful daughter, Camm Nye,
who is the loving mother of my two precious
grandchildren, Petra and Peter

Acknowledgments

This book is the result of the work of many people. My job was just to take the words and weave them into an interesting story—an interesting but true story.

There are so many to thank: lawyers, law officers, doctors, nurses, court reporters, photographers, those who played smaller yet still critical roles in putting this book together.

Deputy Jerry Bailey was extremely generous in helping me research the Texas murders.

Ricklin Pierce was willing to reveal his fears, his human foibles, those things that most of us desperately hide, so that this story could be told.

Earlene Nicholson, the reference librarian at the Finney County Library in Garden City, provided me with copies of the Kansas news releases. Bobbi Morelle, librarian of the *Lubbock Avalanche Journal*, helped me get copies of the Texas stories.

Chester Marston, of Marston Photographic Services in Lubbock, did miracles with tattered old photographs. Because of his amazing work, you will see the faces of those who were part of this story, including six of the seven dead children.

Garden City police captains Charlie Armentrout and James Hawkins helped in ways too numerous to mention. Garden City private investigator Mario Tursini helped pull loose ends together when I ran into roadblocks.

Then there are those who helped once the writing was finished: James Hawkins; his wife, Shelley; Mike Utz; Eva Vachal; and Ricklin Pierce. They spent even more time poring over the manuscript, checking for accuracy, and correcting errors.

My talented editor, Michaela Hamilton, took the corrected manuscript and did a first-rate job of sculpting it into a very good book.

There are also those without whose support I could never have finished this work: Parmer County Sheriff Rex Williams, Gwyn Wilson, Becky and Ray Hinserlow, Larry Elliott, David Cleveland, Dr. Murray Havens, Teri Havens, Dr. Dorothy McWhorter, Dave Buswell, Leonard "Rabbit" Fallin, and my daughter, Camm Nye.

And there are others, many others to whom I'm also grateful. Thank you all for your help.

Preface

I was watching the five o'clock news at my home in Lubbock, Texas, when I first saw Diana Lumbrera. It was June 1991, and she was being escorted out of the local courthouse by two deputy sheriffs.

The newscaster said she had just been charged with the murder of her two-month-old son, José Luís, a crime that had taken place at the Methodist Hospital in Lubbock thirteen years earlier. It was when he said José Luís was only one of seven children whom she had apparently murdered that I sat up and listened.

I'd been a jailer, a street cop, a vice and narcotics undercover operative, a college professor of criminal justice, and a writer of true crime stories. But in all my experiences with crime, criminals, and the "system," I'd never met a serial baby killer. I felt as though man's inhumanity to man had just reached a new low.

In the months that followed, I dug into the facts of all seven deaths, wondering if there was any value in making the story into a book. I wanted to know not only why a woman would commit such hideously evil acts but also why her first six murders had gone undetected for so many years. What I learned shocked, frightened, and infuriated me.

I decided to write this book to shake things up, to challenge those in power to listen to their moral conscience and make the changes necessary to protect the children—all the children.

—Mary Lou Cavenaugh

The names of some of the people involved in this story have been changed to protect their identities.

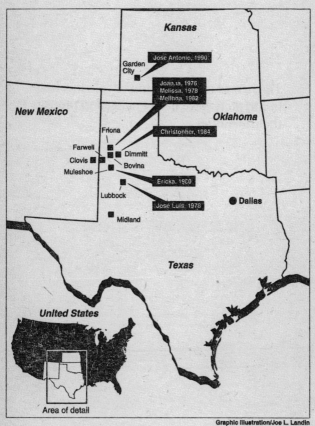

Kansas

Jose Antonio, 1990

Garden City

New Mexico

Joanna, 1976
Melissa, 1978
Melinda, 1982

Oklahoma

Friona

Christopher, 1984

Farwell

Dimmitt

Clovis

Bovina

Muleshoe

Ericka, 1980

Lubbock

Jose Luis, 1978

Dallas

Midland

Texas

United States

Area of detail

Graphic Illustration/Joe L. Landin

Contents

PART I

THE KANSAS INVESTIGATION

Chapter 1

A hundred years ago Garden City was a watering hole along one of the great cattle trails of the Kansas plains, a place where Texas cowboys rested their herds for the night while they drank up their wages in rowdy saloons. Today Garden City is a small, bustling, cosmopolitan community, a place of churches and schools and multicultural neighborhoods where families live and children thrive. On the outskirts of town are cattle feedlots, slaughterhouses, and large grain farms—all part of the legacy of Garden City's colorful past. And at its very center, amid narrow residential streets lined with large Siberian elms, is St. Catherine's, the town's only hospital. It was in the emergency room at St. Catherine's on the night of May 1, 1990, that a bizarre call came through.

Nurse Ann Marie Johnson was sitting at the reception desk, and she responded: "Emergency room, this is Ann."

"My baby's not breathing—his lips are blue—I

found him on the bed," came the hysterical voice of a woman.

"Where are you?"

"My house," replied the woman, her voice dropping to a whisper.

"What is your address?" Ann asked anxiously.

But the only response was the sound of the phone dropping to the floor. Ann screamed into the phone, desperate for a reply, but there was none. She could hear only the muffled sounds of someone moving about in the background—and then nothing.

Ann took a deep breath and looked at her watch; it was exactly 9:40. She spun the chair around and signaled to the dispatcher in the next room to trace the call, then waited nervously, making sure the line stayed open.

Dr. Lauren Welch, a private physician in his mid-thirties, was standing nearby. When he heard the fear in Ann's voice, he walked quickly over to the desk and listened while she quietly repeated to him what the woman had said. As the seconds ticked by, his own anxiety grew. He began to fidget nervously with the metal stethoscope that hung down the front of his gray business suit.

The large crowd of patients seated in the reception area had also heard Ann, and they whispered among themselves, wondering what had caused the young nurse to become so upset.

Ann sat stiffly in her chair, her thoughts racing as she tried to figure out how this call had gone wrong. It occurred to her that it was odd for an emergency call to come through the hospital's switchboard. She looked up at Dr. Welch. "You know, that call came through our switchboard. That means she had to find our number first, then dial it. Yet she was too upset to remember her address. That's very strange. Why didn't she just call 9-1-1 and get an ambulance? At least then there'd be a computer visual of her address. I just don't get it."

Then, as more moments passed, Ann worried about how she had handled the call. She reproached herself for not getting the woman's name or address or phone number, and she prayed that they would find this child in time.

Telephone calls that come through switchboards cannot be traced directly by the police. A more lengthy process involving a national networking system has to be used, and while the dispatcher was working frantically to get this process started, Ann and Dr. Welch kept their eyes fixed on the front entrance to the emergency room. They hoped that the woman would soon come running in with the child.

Eight minutes after Ann received that call, an attractive dark-haired woman in her early thirties rushed through the glass doors with a four-year-old boy hanging limply in her arms. It was exactly 9:48.

"My baby's dying!" she screamed as she raced past the desk and through the doors leading to the E.R. trauma rooms. She seemed to know exactly where she was going.

Greatly relieved, Ann hung up the phone, bolted out of her chair, and reached the woman as she cleared the doors. She grabbed the woman's shoulder. "This way," she ordered, directing her into the first trauma room. "Here, let me have him." Ann grabbed the child, laid him on the steel table in the center of the large, well-lighted room, and began giving him cardiopulmonary resuscitation (CPR).

Dr. Welch rushed into the room behind them. He ran to the red metal crash cart on the far wall, jerked open the drawer, and began pulling out the equipment they would need.

Betty Woodward, a motherly nurse in her early thirties, was in a nearby room when the commotion started. She stepped out into the hallway and saw Ann and Dr. Welch working on the boy. She raced to the trauma room, grabbed the wall telephone and put out a Code Blue announcement.

"Emergency Room Code Blue—Room Four," she said as calmly as she could manage. Then she hung up the phone, tilted the child's head back to make sure the throat was clear, and began giving him mouth-to-mouth resuscitation.

Dr. Michael Shull, an attractive, boyish-looking pediatrician in his mid-thirties, had just sat down in the office area and was loosening his tie as he prepared to dictate some notes.

"Doctor," yelled someone in an urgent voice, "there's a Code Blue on a child in Room Four."

Shull jumped to his feet and raced to the room as Betty Woodward's announcement came over the loudspeaker. He knew he would be in charge of the Code Blue because he was the only pediatrician in the E.R. at that time.

As the doctors and nurses worked frantically on

the child, others ran in to help. One was a female technician, who noticed the child's mother leaning against the far wall, softly pleading for them to save her baby. The technician went to the mother, put her arm reassuringly around the woman's shoulders, and led her gently out of the room. She felt tremendous compassion for this poor mother, because she had seen other parents who had lost children, and she knew that nothing could be worse.

As they worked, Ann told the rest of the team what the mother had said about finding the child unconscious on his bed. While the nurses continued the CPR and respirations, one doctor removed the child's little blue sweater and jeans while the other checked his vital signs. A quick examination of his entire body was made.

The child was small for his age, he was not breathing, and he had no pulse or heartbeat. His pupils were fixed at three to four millimeters (an indication of brain damage); his core body temperature (rectal temperature) was 96 degrees, more than 2 degrees below normal; and he was cyanotic (blue in color from lack of oxygen). His skin was becoming mottled (pinkish-gray in certain areas), which indicated that the pooling of blood in the lowest portions of his body tissues had already begun.

It was obvious that the child was probably too far gone to save, but if there was any chance of bringing him back, they wanted to try. Injections of heart stimulants were given, a cardiac monitor was attached, and a respiratory bag was positioned over his face. More technicians from auxiliary departments ran in to do their assigned tasks. Someone from the lab drew blood samples, a radiology technician brought in a portable machine and took X rays, and a cardiopulmonary technician took charge of the ambu-bag (a portable respirator with an inflated bag attached to a face mask).

Soon muscles ached, beads of sweat ran down worried faces, and minds struggled to determine what had caused the child's condition.

As the team worked, they all noticed two things. The first was the boy's cyanosis (the blue color of his skin), which was a sign that something had prevented oxygen from getting into his bloodstream. The second was the large number of petechiae (pronounced pa-*teek*-e-i) that covered his face, forehead, and eyelids.

Dr. Welch focused on the petechiae, and with a deep note of concern in his voice he said, "This child's been vomiting a lot."

Petechiae are pinpoint hemorrhages in the skin that appear as little red or reddish-purple spots. Two things can cause these tiny hemorrhages. The most common cause is a back-flow or buildup of pressure within the vascular system so great that little holes break open in the capillaries, the tiny blood vessels in the skin. This lets bits of blood push out, which causes red spots to appear. An example would be the pressure caused by vomiting, but only severe vomiting could have caused the numerous petechiae that were showing on this child's face. Another, less common cause of petechiae is the direct damage to the capillary walls that sometimes results from massive bacterial or viral infections.

The medical team logically guessed that the petechiae were related to the cyanosis of the boy's skin; that is, something had prevented him from breathing, and the resulting pressure had caused the petechial ruptures to occur. It made sense that if he had been vomiting severely, then some of the vomitus had probably entered and blocked the air passages. Clearing any obstructions from the air passages was Dr. Shull's first priority.

He selected a plastic tube about the size of the child's smallest finger, inserted it, and pushed it gently down into the lungs. To his amazement, he encountered no obstructions.

"His airway is completely clear," he announced in his quiet voice. "There's only a thread of mucus here, and he could easily have coughed that up." So what had blocked the child's air passages?

Shull quickly selected a second tube, a nasogastric tube, which he inserted through the child's nose and pushed down into his stomach. He did this because the child had been given mouth-to-mouth resuscitation before the mask and bag had been put in place. Mouth-to-mouth resuscitation often causes air to be forced into the stomach, and when the stomach is distended, it is more difficult to inflate the lungs. The insertion of the naso-gastric tube rectifies this condition by releasing the trapped air.

But there was also a second reason. When someone who has stopped breathing and has no heart activity is resuscitated, vomiting often follows, creating a risk that vomitus will get into the trachea and prevent breathing. To avoid this problem, the nasogastric tube is inserted to catch anything coming up from the stomach.

When the tube reached the child's stomach, undigested food material came back up.

"There's food coming back up!" said Dr. Shull with surprise. "This child hasn't been vomiting at all."

This information was significant. Since the child hadn't been vomiting and since there was nothing in the air passages to prevent breathing, then a massive infection must have caused the petechiae on the child's face and neck. Such an infection was the only other natural reason for their presence.

At that moment a middle-aged nurse rushed into the room carrying the child's hospital record. She looked around to see whose hands might be free and handed the folder to Dr. Welch. He thanked her and flipped it open with his thumb, looking first at the last entry. It was dated the night before, April 30, 1990.

"This child was seen by Dr. Gaines just last night," he said slowly, paraphrasing what he was reading. "According to this record the mother complained that the child was having severe abdominal pain and vomiting, so they did a complete physical on him, including a complete blood count, urinalysis, and a three-way abdominal [two abdominal X rays and one chest X ray]." He paused for a moment.

"Wait a minute," he said, staring at the chart, a note of confusion in his voice. "Except for a slight respiratory infection, everything showed normal. Even his blood count was only 20,200. Gaines prescribed some amoxicillin, but with this blood count it wasn't really necessary."

Dr. Welch looked up abruptly at Dr. Shull. "You know, this was a normal exam the boy had. I wouldn't have even put him on an antibiotic."

A heavy silence filled the room as each person tried to make some sense out of what they had just learned. Yet none of it made sense.

They knew the child hadn't vomited—his stomach was still full of food. And now they knew that he hadn't had a significant infection; the proof of that was in the tests that had been done on him the night before. So something else must have prevented him from breathing—but what?

Then a very ugly thought began to intrude. They had been looking for natural causes, but what if the cause of this child's condition wasn't natural?

Dr. Welch felt a sudden shiver as he remembered an article in a medical journal he had once read. The article had been about smothering. It had said that smothering could create the kind of pressure on the vascular system that resulted in petechiae, specifically in the pattern that was showing on this child's face and neck.

When a child's breathing is obstructed, the heart keeps pumping blood through the vascular system, but the lungs stop, so no oxygen reaches the cells. The child experiences what is called "air hunger."

He or she feels a growing need to breathe along with a sharp burning sensation in the chest. The child will struggle desperately for air as the heart beats faster and faster in an attempt to obtain the life-giving oxygen the body must have. Then, when the pressure on the vascular system is the greatest, tiny petechial ruptures occur in the thinnest tissues on the face and neck.

After a couple of minutes of violent, terrifying struggle, the child will finally lose consciousness, but the heart will continue to beat until the residue of oxygen runs out. This will take another two or three minutes, then the point of death is reached. If the child is not resuscitated within this five-minute period after breathing is blocked, he or she will die.

That was the horrifying picture forming in Dr. Welch's mind. He realized that the child must have been suffocated; that much was obvious from the cyanosis. But how? A child of this age couldn't possibly have suffocated accidentally unless he had become trapped in some kind of airtight container, like a refrigerator. But the mother had said that she had found him unconscious on a bed. That left only one other possibility. This was no accident. Someone had smothered the child.

Dr. Welch was the only one willing to put his thoughts into words. "You don't suppose somebody did this to him, do you?" he asked incredulously, looking directly at Dr. Shull.

His colleague met his gaze. "It almost looks like it, doesn't it?" he said, unable to keep his mind from racing toward the same conclusion. It was the only thing Michael Shull could think to say. The emptiness he was feeling at that moment had swallowed up all the other words.

Ann Marie Johnson listened to the doctors as she continued her work, but she had her own questions. She remembered that strange phone call the child's mother had made and her unusual response when asked for her address. She wondered if the mother could have done this, and then she wondered: Why?

Betty Woodward kept her eyes on the equipment and tried hard not to think. She reminded herself that this was Garden City, Kansas, a small midwestern town where people protected their children; they didn't hurt them. And she reminded herself that nobody would ever intentionally kill a child—certainly not a mother.

The team continued its efforts until 10:25. They had spent a total of thirty-seven minutes working on the child, mostly because it was so difficult to accept the fact that he was gone. Then Dr. Shull paused and looked up at the others. He didn't have to say anything. They all knew. It was a battle that had been lost.

Losing a patient is always sad, and especially so when the patient is a small child. But the questions raised by this boy's death made them feel far worse than they could ever have imagined. As they finished their duties, each of them tried to deal with his or her own feelings of grief—and outrage. Then Dr. Shull turned to the nurses and made a simple but important request: "Please take the time to make personal notes about everything you saw and did on this code tonight as soon as you can."

Everyone except Dr. Shull and Nurse Woodward left the room. They stayed to clean the child up so that his mother could be brought back in to see him one last time. They knew the tubes would have to be left in his small body, because the coroner would have to be called and an autopsy ordered. Removing the tubes would destroy any evidence left behind in the throat or nasal passages.

Ten minutes later Dr. Shull went out to tell the young mother than her son was dead. The woman's name was Diana Lumbrera, and her son was José Antonio Lumbrera.

This was the part of his job that Michael Shull hated. It was difficult under any circumstances to tell parents that their child had died, because it caused them so much pain. But parents always wanted to know *why* the death had occurred. That simple question made this situation especially difficult for him, because he wasn't certain why José had died. He wouldn't know that until after the autopsy was performed.

He found Diana leaning back on a faded green vinyl couch in the small office of the supervising nurse, Mattie Johnson. A young man and woman, obviously friends of Diana's, were in the room with her. Diana's eyes were shut, and she looked tired, but as soon as the doctor entered, she stood up, nervously tucked the fingers of her right hand into the right rear pocket of her tight jeans, and waited.

"I'm very sorry," he said gently as he looked into

her dark eyes, "but we weren't able to save your son."

Diana hesitated, then covered her face with her hands and began to cry. Suddenly she collapsed backward, apparently unconscious.

Shull lunged forward, grabbed her upper body, and eased her slowly onto the couch. Suddenly her body began to tremble with some kind of seizure, causing her left arm and leg to jerk uncontrollably.

"See if she has a medical record here," Shull ordered the nurse, "and if she does, bring it to me as quickly as possible." The doctor hadn't expected such an unusual reaction. He thought Diana might have a serious medical condition that would require immediate attention.

Locating a patient's record takes time, so while a search was being made, a priest and a nun came to comfort Diana. They prayed with her, and when she felt better, they carefully helped her into a wheelchair and took her and her two friends back into Room Four. Dr. Shull, Betty Woodward, and Ann Marie Johnson were already waiting there when she arrived.

Diana looked at the body for a moment, then brought her hands up over her face and began to sob loudly. A few seconds passed, then she suddenly fainted, her body going limp in the chair. Dr. Shull moved quickly to her side and checked her eyes while one of the nurses took her pulse. But before anything else could be done, Diana came back to consciousness. She pulled her body up straight in the chair, leaned forward and touched the child's body, then began crying once again. Shull and the nurse stepped back and waited.

As the moments ticked by, everyone stood in silence, awkwardly watching the scene, not knowing what to do. Then Betty Woodward suggested that they say a rosary for the child. It was in the midst of this rosary that the doctor and nurses became aware of three very strange things.

First was the fact that Diana barely touched her son's body. Experience had taught these medical professionals that most loving parents became very emotional at the sight of their child's dead body and would hold, hug, and kiss it until someone gently forced them to leave. But not Diana. Why?

Second was the way in which she was crying. She made very loud but level-pitched sobs, not the normal kind of up-and-down, loud-to soft sobs that a person makes when genuinely grieving.

And third was the absence of tears. During the rosary, Ann Marie picked up a box of facial tissues and started to hand them to Diana, but she noticed that in spite of all the sobbing, the woman's eyes and face were completely dry.

After the rosary the priest and nun wheeled Diana back to the small office, but when Dr. Shull looked for her a few minutes later, he found her standing outside in the night air, smoking a cigarette and talking to her friends.

He still didn't want to believe that her child had been murdered; in his mind he continued to search for another reasonable explanation for the death. He hoped that something would make sense if he could only get enough information. He offered Diana his sympathies once again, then gently asked if she could tell him about José's recent health history. He said it was important that he know or he wouldn't have asked at a time like this.

She looked up at him, her face a mask of grief, and slowly nodded her head in understanding. She took a deep breath and looked off into the distance, then began to tell her story.

She said José had become sick the day before, on Monday, April 30. He had thrown up all day and had complained of having pains in his stomach and leg. His condition got so bad that she rushed him to this same emergency room, where he was examined and given some medicine.

The doctor told her to give José a dose of the medicine as soon as she returned home, then to give him the rest today, which she had done. But José had become even sicker; he continued to throw up, and he had a high fever and refused to eat anything. By early evening she became so worried that she telephoned the hospital for advice, and a nurse told her to bathe him and to get his head wet so that his fever would come down. She went into the bedroom to get him, but he was asleep, and she decided that it was best to let him rest.

Later, when she went in to check on him again, she discovered that he wasn't breathing. She immediately called the hospital, but when the woman in the emergency room kept asking her questions, she dropped the phone and raced the child to the hospital herself.

Dr. Shull watched Diana carefully as she talked, and he didn't miss the fact that except for her facial expressions, she displayed very little emotion when talking about her dead child. Nor did he miss the fact that she said her son had been throwing up all day—he knew that the child's stomach had been full of undigested food.

When she finished her story, he thanked her, then walked back inside, even more frustrated and upset than before. Nurse Mattie Johnson was waiting for him at the reception desk. She handed him Diana Lumbrera's medical file.

The file was a legal-size manila folder stuffed with papers that had been clipped together at the top. And only fate could have intervened to orchestrate what happened next. Shull arbitrarily flipped the file open near the back, and the first record he saw was a social service report dated February 1986. It had been written at the time of José's birth.

The report said that Diana had given birth to five other children in Texas, all of whom had subsequently died. The cause of death for some was "seizures," and for others it was "SIDS" (sudden infant death syndrome). The doctor was stunned. He knew the record couldn't be accurate, because six children in one family just didn't die of things like that.

When Dr. Shull finished reading the file, he closed it and handed it back to the nurse, his anxiety obvious. "I want you to put this record away where no one can find it for now," he whispered. "I don't want *anyone* looking at it."

Shull realized that José's death might be a homicide. If it was, he didn't want to make any mistakes. It was important to prevent any bias from forming in the minds of those who had participated in the Code Blue.

Then he went to the dictaphone and put everything he had seen, heard, and done on tape to be transcribed later. He would see Diana twice more before she left the hospital, and each time she would add something new to her story. It was close to midnight when the doctor learned one last bit of troubling information. One of the nurses noticed him sitting by the dictaphone and was concerned by how exhausted he looked. She stopped to talk to him, and during their brief conversation, she mentioned something Diana Lumbrera had told her earlier in the evening.

Diana had said that she had found her son not breathing when she went to check on him at nine o'clock. But Dr. Shull remembered clearly that the Code Blue had started at exactly 9:48. Why had Diana waited more than forty minues to get help after discovering that her child wasn't breathing?

For many people the next step would have been easy: they would have gone to a telephone and called the police. But Michael Shull was a cautious man who always took great care to ensure that what he did was correct. He had to be certain, so he went over everything once again in his mind.

He knew that four-year-old children died only of natural illnesses, fatal genetic defects, serious injuries caused by accidents, or severe damage caused by some form of child abuse. This child's medical records showed that he was too healthy to have died of a natural illness, and there were no obvious signs of an accidental injury or abuse on his body—except the petechiae. And the presence of those petechiae wouldn't be explained even if a genetic-related defect had caused the child's death. So what else was there to think except that the child had been smothered?

But Dr. Shull also knew that mistakes were sometimes made. So, what if the results of the tests that had been made on the child the night before were incorrect? What if the child had actually died of a massive infection? But what about his cyanotic condition? Something had prevented him from breathing, but nothing had been lodged in his throat, nor was it swollen.

Plus, there was his mother's strange behavior to consider and the inconsistencies in the stories she had told. And the mysterious deaths of her other five children. But could a mother really kill her child in cold blood? Or would she protect someone else who had done such a monstrous thing?

Most of all, Dr. Shull knew that he wasn't 100 percent sure the child had been murdered; only the autopsy could determine that. And even if the boy had been murdered, there was no proof that his mother had done it. Surely to contact the police now would be equal to accusing her of killing her son. So how would he feel if he did accuse her, only to discover later that he was wrong? But on the other hand, what if he did nothing and she *had* actually murdered the boy?

There were other young patients in the emergency room who needed Shull's attention, and as he treated them he continued to mull these facts over. He was desperate to find an easy answer—but there wasn't one.

He debated with himself until nearly five o'clock in the morning, when one pertinent fact finally settled the matter. If it was murder, the police would want to begin their investigation by attending the autopsy, and that was scheduled to begin in less than four hours. With a heavy heart he picked up the phone and dialed the Garden City Police Department.

"I need to speak to a detective."

Chapter 2

The autopsy room was large, well lighted, and cold. It was filled with steel counters, glass and metal jars, steel instruments, sinks, and scales. Freshly scrubbed tile covered the walls and floor, and the pungent odor of strong antiseptics permeated the air. An air-conditioning unit set high on one wall provided a soft, steady hum.

The child's naked body lay on a large steel table in the center of the room. Around the table were gathered a group of police officers and college students, who had been invited to attend the autopsy as part of a local forensic science seminar.

Dr. Eva Vachal slipped a thin plastic apron over her green suit, pulled on strong rubber gloves, and moved through the circle to the child's side. She was a small, quiet woman in her mid-thirties who was employed by the hospital as a general pathologist.

There are two kinds of autopsies. One is the usual hospital kind, which is performed by a general pathologist who is searching for the ravages of disease that caused the person's natural death. The other is the forensic kind, which is performed by a forensic pathologist who is searching for the cause of the person's unnatural death—whether by suicide, homicide, or accident. These two types of autopsies differ significantly, and if a crime is involved, the forensic approach is better suited to determine the exact cause and manner of death. That information becomes extremely important in the prosecution of the crime.

Because of the suspicious circumstances surrounding the death of José Lumbrera, Dr. Vachal tried to contact Dr. William G. Eckert, a famous forensic pathologist who lived in Wichita, Kansas, to see if he would be interested in joining her in the autopsy. However, Dr. Eckert had been called unexpectedly to testify in an unrelated case in another state, so Dr. Vachal would have to perform the procedure by herself. She had little forensic training, and she could feel the nervousness in the pit of her stomach as she began.

She switched on the overhead tape recorder and first made a thorough external examination of the child's entire body. Every feature and mark were noted, including age, height, weight, hair and eye color. A search for any moles, scars, skin lesions, or bruises revealed only a few small scars around the knees, the kind typically seen on a small, active child.

She carefully examined his hands and fingernails for any foreign material such as blood, skin, or clothing fibers that would indicate a struggle had taken place with an assailant. She found nothing. The only apparent abnormality was the presence of numerous petechiae on his face, eyelids, forehead, and neck. Finally, X rays were taken, followed by photographs of the body.

Next, Dr. Vachal performed an internal examination of the body. To enter the body cavity, she carefully made a large Y incision extending across the chest from shoulder to shoulder, then continuing down the front of the abdomen to the pubis. It was a gruesome sight for the uninitiated, and some of the observers found it difficult to watch.

The doctor worked slowly and meticulously so that she would miss nothing. As she reached inside, her first observation was that her rubber gloves did not stick to the organs. That meant the child had not been dehydrated, so it was unlikely that he had suffered from a high fever or vomiting just before his death.

She moved to the neck and spine: nothing abnormal was noted. Next came the chest cavity: no rib fractures. The heart and lungs were removed, examined, and weighed. The lungs showed small areas of recent hemorrhage—an interesting clue—but everything else appeared normal. Fluid samples and small tissue sections were taken for microscopic analysis, which she would perform later. Then the esophagus and trachea were removed and examined; they were undamaged, with no obvious signs of disease.

Next came the abdomen and then the pelvis: no signs of trauma. Again, each of the organs was removed and examined, followed by the collection of tissue samples for later analysis. Everything appeared normal. The stomach contained a considerable amount of undigested food substance, which meant that Dr. Shull had been correct: this child had not vomited prior to his death.

A urine sample was taken to detect the presence of any drugs in the body. Along with blood and gastric samples, it would be sent to the forensic laboratory of the Kansas Bureau of Investigation in Topeka for analysis.

Finally the head and brain were examined. Dr. Vachal had already noted the large amount of petechiae on the face and neck, but when she examined the eyes and eyelids, she made a startling discovery. In the right eye the conjunctiva—the mucous membrane that lines the inside of the eyelids and the forepart of the eyeball—showed an unusual linear hemorrhage, another important clue. The remainder of her examination uncovered no further injuries or abnormalities.

Before the autopsy had begun, a troubled Dr. Shull had gone to Dr. Vachal's office and told her about the Code Blue on the child the night before. He had also told her about the deaths of Diana's other five children so that she would be especially alert for any signs of a genetic disorder that might have caused the child's death.

He was anxious to hear her results, so she agreed to page him when she was finished. After speaking with Dr. Vachal, he walked back to his medical office, which was in a pediatrics clinic a block down the street. But Shull wasn't able to concentrate on his work; his mind was preoccupied with the autopsy that was under way. He finally instructed his nurse to cancel his remaining appointments for the day and rushed back to the hospital.

Dr. Vachal was just finishing the procedure as he slipped quietly into the room. He stood to the side and waited nervously until the others had left, but he could tell just from her expression that the news wasn't good. He was right. Her findings indicated that the child had been smothered.

Chapter 3

Detective Ken Elliott of the Garden City Police Department turned the unmarked car left onto Tonio Street, while Detective James Hawkins checked the report for the exact address. It was somewhere in the 2300 block—two blocks farther down. The two detectives knew this northwestern section of town. It was made up mostly of small neighborhoods lined with cheaply built houses and apartment buildings. And considering its age, it was remarkably clean; even the streets and gutters were clean.

They spotted the address on the left—a small, box-shaped duplex at the back of a deep empty lot. Diana's white compact car was parked on the hard dirt drive next to the front door. Elliott pulled up to the curb and parked.

Ken Elliott was a tall, thirty-year-old bachelor with perfect posture and a taste for expensive clothes. He normally handled all cases involving crimes against children, so he had been assigned to investigate the possible homicide of the four-year-old child.

James Hawkins was an intelligent, soft-spoken former schoolteacher in his mid-thirties who had been assigned to assist Elliott. Hawkins was as light-hearted and humorous as Elliott was serious and intense.

The two men represented half of the four-man detective division in the small but progressive Garden City Police Department. Hawkins had been a detective longer than Elliott, but both were well trained and good at their jobs.

Neither detective had been able to attend the autopsy, so they had waited until now—two days after the child's death—to make their first contact with Diana Lumbrera. They had already talked to Dr. Shull and obtained a copy of the autopsy report from Dr. Vachal. Now it was time to see the home in which the child had lived and to hear his mother's story about the way he had died.

The detectives walked to the front door and knocked. Thirty seconds later they were admitted by Diana's roommate, a woman in her mid-thirties named Marguerite. As they walked into the small living room, they saw Diana sitting on a dark brown couch. She was dressed in tight jeans and a black turtleneck sweater, and beside her sat her current boyfriend, a darkly handsome male who appeared to be in his late twenties. Diana introduced him as Thomas. The roommate and the boyfriend sat in silence and watched.

Elliott was surprised by what he saw. Diana was an attractive woman who was close to his own age. She had dark, shiny, shoulder-length hair, deep brown eyes, and a nicely shaped body. He guessed that she was probably five feet six in height. Her apartment was clean, well organized, and nicely furnished, and everything was neatly in its place. It wasn't what he had expected.

"Ms. Lumbrera, we know this is a sad time for you," Elliott said, after introducing himself and his partner, "but we'd like to ask you a few questions about your son, if you don't mind. It won't take long, I promise."

"Okay," she replied. She remained seated, but it was obvious that she was surprised by their visit. She had on very little makeup, and there was a distinct pallor to her face, which made her look tired. Even her voice sounded tired—tired and sad—as she answered the detective.

Elliott and Hawkins sat down on overstuffed chairs, and Elliott took out his pen and notebook. He began by asking Diana about where she was from, and she said she had been born in northern Texas, in a little farm town called Friona. She explained that she had moved around quite a bit, living in a number of places in Texas, then later in New Mexico, and finally here in Kansas. She had arrived in Garden City in 1985, shortly after her mother had died of cancer. When asked, she explained that her mother's cancer was the only serious illness in her family's history.

"Where do you work, Ms. Lumbrera?" Elliott asked.

Diana said she was employed at the Monfort Beef Packing Company, a local slaughterhouse and processing plant east of town. She worked as an inspector on the "B" shift (4:30 P.M. to 12:30 A.M.), and her roommate and boyfriend also worked there, on the same shift.

"Could you please tell us what happened on the day *before* José died—Monday, April 30?"

Diana paused and looked down at her hands for a moment, then slowly began to recount the events of that day.

As she talked, Elliott took notes and listened intently for any differences from the version she had told Dr. Shull. Her story was essentially the same. She had left José at the baby-sitter's and gone to work. Later that afternoon, she received a call from the baby-sitter saying that José had become very ill. She left work immediately, picked up the child, and rushed him to the hospital emergency room. Along the way he became nauseous, so she stopped the car, and he vomited into the gutter.

"Exactly where did you pull over?" Elliott inquired.

With a puzzled look on her face, she answered that it had been by the Coastal Mart, a small convenience store near the intersection of Jenny Barker Road and Highway 50. The detectives would conduct a thorough search of that gutter days later and would find no evidence of any vomit.

"And what is your baby-sitter's name?"

Diana paused and repositioned her body on the couch, then answered that she couldn't remember.

That didn't make sense. What mother would forget her baby-sitter's name after only two days? Elliott wondered why she was trying to keep this information from him. He gently pushed her for an answer. "Okay. Then how do you get there in your car? Which way do you drive?"

Diana ran her hand through her dark hair and closed her eyes for a moment, as if she was feeling faint. Then she slowly described the route she always took. Later that afternoon Hawkins would drive that route and find the woman who had babysat José just hours before his death.

As the interview continued, Diana became increasingly nervous. She seemed not to understand why police officers had come to her home and why they were asking her so many questions.

"Tell us about the next day," Elliott said, "the day that José died."

Diana slowly explained that she and her son had slept late that day and had awakened about noon. She had felt that that was unusual because José usually got up early no matter how he felt. Then she told them what he had said to her, so that they would understand. "He said he didn't feel good, and he said, 'Mama, don't go to work today. Please, Mama, let's stay home.'"

Diana described how she had tried to make him eat something, and she said that for two days he had refused any food. She said that during that time he kept throwing up yellow stuff.

Elliott glanced at Hawkins. She was still lying about her child's refusal to eat food in the hours before his death. Why would she do that if she wasn't trying to hide something?

Diana continued her story, her eyes cast downward, her voice soft and sad. She said she had known that José felt really bad that day, because he kept clinging to her. She dropped him off at the baby-sitter's at the regular time, but once she arrived at the plant, she became so worried about him that she returned immediately to the baby-sitter's house, picked him up, and took him straight home.

When they got home, she put him on her bed and lay down with him until he fell asleep. Then she got up and watched TV for a while.

She said she had continued to worry about him because his fever was high, so at seven o'clock she called the hospital for advice. A nurse told her to bathe him and to make sure his head got wet. She went into the bedroom to get him, but he was asleep, so she decided to let him rest for a while.

She described how she had gone in to check on him again at nine o'clock and had found him unconscious in the darkened room. When she quickly turned on the lamp by the side of the bed, she saw that his lips were bluish. That frightened her. She screamed, "Baby, wake up! What's wrong with you?" but he didn't awaken. She said she had immediately called the hospital.

Elliott and Hawkins hadn't missed her statement about finding the child unconscious at nine o'clock. That was the same time she had mentioned to Dr. Shull, and it left 48 minutes between the time she found the child unconscious and the time she arrived at the emergency room. Yet her apartment was no more than ten minutes from St. Catherine's Hospital.

They wondered what had happened in those missing forty or so minutes. Why had she waited so long to get help for her dying son? But they didn't mention that now; it was something they would pursue at a later time.

Diana finished her story, saying that she had rushed José to the hospital in her car. Then she added her thoughts on what had caused his death. She said she guessed that he might have had appendicitis, because she had once had appendicitis and his symptoms were similar.

"Ms. Lumbrera, who was with you here in this apartment on May 1, the day José died?" Elliott asked.

She replied that she had been home alone with her son. Marguerite and Thomas had gone to work at four o'clock that afternoon, and no one else had been there.

When asked if she knew of anyone else who might have wanted to hurt her child, she said no. She explained that José was a very good son, a beautiful child who loved his mother and whom everyone loved.

"Do you have any other children?" It was Hawkins' turn to ask the questions. He asked them softly, kindly, taking in every nuance in her voice and body language.

"No," she replied, in a voice barely louder than a whisper. She moved back against the couch and crossed her arms in front of her. Hawkins noticed the subtle signs that told him this question had made her feel even more threatened.

"Have you ever had any other children?" he gently pursued.

Diana hesitated, not sure of how she should respond. "I once had others," she said without expression. Then instantly she erupted in anger, "The newspaper said I had five other children who had died!" she said indignantly, as if that were a lie.

Hawkins wondered if her reaction was really anger or simply a diversion. He thought it might be fear masked to look like anger. "Could you tell us about them?" he continued, ignoring her outburst.

The detectives could see that she didn't want to talk about the other deaths, so they just sat there, looking at her and waiting for her to answer. The long silence increased her discomfort, and she began to squirm slightly. She bent over and brushed an imagined spot from her right pant leg, obviously stalling for time until she could think of the right thing to say.

Finally, in a very small voice she said that her other children had all become sick and died while she was still living in Texas.

"What were their names, and when did they die?" Hawkins asked. More seconds passed, then Diana slowly began to recite partial names and approximate dates. Her unusual response was not lost on the detectives. It was not the kind that one would expect from a grieving mother.

As the interview continued, the two detectives weighed whether this frightened young woman had, in fact, murdered her four-year-old son. She seemed to be an ordinary person, someone unable to commit a premeditated murder. Could the child's death possibly have been accidental? Could she simply have failed to fully explain the facts to the doctors? Or could she be covering up for someone else who had murdered the child? Could someone else have murdered him as an act of revenge on her? Could it be that she was simply too frightened to tell the truth?

Of course, they had to consider the inconsistencies in her stories and her blatant lies about José's refusal to eat and his supposed bouts of vomiting. Also to be factored in was her reluctance to provide the information they requested.

Something else, though, seemed to be askew. Diana was clearly trying to convey an image of being a hardworking mother who had struggled to raise her son the right way and who was now dealing with the tragedy of his death. But just as Dr. Shull had mentioned, her emotions didn't fit the circumstances. The detectives could sense her fear, but where was her grief? She didn't shed a single tear while talking about her six dead children.

They finished the interview and asked Diana if she would mind showing them the rest of her house.

She quickly agreed. She led them into her bedroom and showed them the oversize waterbed on which she had found José unconscious two nights earlier. Next she showed them the toilet in the adjacent bathroom where he had vomited so many times on the day of his death. Then she led them through the rest of the house, ending the tour, which seemed to make her feel better.

She thought they were finished, but they weren't. Elliott asked her if he could take some photographs of the apartment and borrow the sheets and the pillowcases which had been on the bed at the time of José's death.

Diana didn't understand why they wanted photos of her home. She didn't realize they were investigating a suspicious death—probably a homicide—and that photographs of the crime scene were a standard requirement. Nor did she realize that lab tests on the bed linens would help to establish whether her story about Jose's having vomited before his death was true. She reluctantly agreed to their requests.

While Elliott took the photos and collected the sheets and pillowcases, Hawkins spoke to the roommate, Marguerite, and the boyfriend, Thomas, about the events surrounding the child's death.

Marguerite said José had been sad and clinging to his mother for affection on the day of his death. She said she had learned of José's death while she was at work, so after she got off she had gone straight to the hospital, but Diana had already gone home.

Thomas said José was sad and also very serious on the day that he died. Thomas seemed very concerned about the reason for the detectives' unexpected visit and the questions they were asking. He wanted them to know that Diana and her son were very close and that they loved each other a great deal.

When the two detectives had finished the questioning, they thanked Diana for her help and left. As they drove back to their office, they discussed the outcome of their visit.

Hawkins, in his usual lighthearted but analytical way, began to ask a series of questions, beginning with, "Well, what do you think she's thinking?"

Then the two men considered the possibilities of the case, one by one. They wondered if Diana had intentionally been trying to steer them in the wrong direction, or if maybe she wasn't intelligent enough to know what she was doing, or if she was so clever that she was actually weaving a web that would ensure her innocence if she were caught.

Clearly they had grounds to be suspicious of her, but no concrete evidence. And one very important question remained unanswered: If Diana had murdered her son, what had been her motive? What could possibly have made a young mother plan and carry out the murder of a four-year-old child, a boy who had no signs of previous physical abuse?

And what about the deaths of her other five children in Texas? Had Diana murdered them, too, and if so, again, *Why?*

Neither Elliott nor Hawkins wanted to believe that such a chain of murders could happen. The whole idea seemed almost too bizarre to consider seriously—except for one thing: they both had a gut feeling that she was guilty.

The detectives drove into the police lot and parked. Their next step was obvious. If the child had been murdered, their only hope of proving it lay in finding enough physical evidence connected to the crime. And since any remaining evidence would probably be in Diana's apartment, they would have to get a search warrant and serve it before she or someone else realized what they were doing and destroyed whatever traces remained.

Chapter 4

St. Mary's Catholic Church was heavy with sadness as the young priest stepped up on the pulpit and looked down at the large congregation. All the pews were completely filled. Diana and her father, brothers, sisters, aunts, uncles, and close friends sat together on the left front side. The rest of the church was filled by strangers who had come to offer their sympathy and support to the child's mother. Everyone tried not to stare at the small white casket, which was set alone at the base of the altar.

The priest went through the ritual of the funeral service. He offered words of comfort to the family, words that spoke of living and dying, of the strength of motherly love, and of the need to carry on. He encouraged them to accept God's decision to take back this beautiful child.

When he finished, those attending formed a long line and walked by the small white casket to view the child's body and say their final good-byes. José was dressed in a miniature pale blue tuxedo, a lacy white shirt, and a red bow tie. A red cummerbund was strapped around his waist, and his raggedy teddy tear was tucked beneath his left arm. The suspicious mass of petechiae was gone from his face; it had disappeared the day before, when his body was embalmed.

Thirty minutes later, a long black hearse led the funeral procession two miles north of town to the Valley View Cemetery, a sprawling, grass-covered field outlined with large shade trees. The mourners gathered in a semicircle and watched in silence as José's small coffin was lowered into a cheap, un-marked grave. Diana sobbed hysterically, then fainted and had to be carried back to her car.

While the child's funeral was in progress, Detectives Elliott and Hawkins were busy collecting the evidence necessary to obtain a search warrant for Diana's apartment. Dr. Vachal's autopsy report would show that a homicide had been committed, but they still needed evidence that would connect Diana to the crime. Because of the urgency involved, their captain, Charlie Armentrout, a former military officer, pitched in to help. The three men divided the work, than set out to interview other possible witnesses, including the medical personnel from St. Catherine's, Diana's neighbors, Diana's baby-sitter, and Diana's supervisor at the Monfort Beef Packing Company. Copies of Diana's and the boy's medical records also had to be picked up.

It was past six when they met back at the Law Enforcement Center (LEC). While Armentrout placed a call to the Texas authorities, Elliott and

Hawkins began typing up the search warrant. When the documents were ready, the two detectives rushed to the Finney County Courthouse to see county attorney Ricklin Pierce. Everyone but Pierce had already left for the day; they found him at work in his office.

Pierce was a thirty-six-year-old bachelor, tall and slim, with thinning dark hair, long seventies side-burns, and gray plastic-rimmed glasses. He was brilliant, shy, and much too sensitive to live comfortably in the political arena of an elected official. Yet he loved being a prosecutor, and he could be a fierce opponent in the courtroom when his passion for justice was unleashed.

Elliott and Hawkins sat across from Pierce and watched as he read through their reports. Elliott glanced at his watch and silently wished that the prosecutor would hurry; it was already six-thirty. He guessed that any evidence left in the Lumbrera apartment would be destroyed if they didn't get that search warrant and serve it soon—very soon. He began to tap his foot nervously on the floor as he watched Pierce pick up the last report.

Pierce pushed the jumble of lawbooks and legal pads to the side of his large desk and stacked the reports in a neat pile in the center. He looked up with an expression of amazement and said, "Do you think *she* killed the boy?"

The two men explained that there was no way to tell, not after the one short interview they had had with her in her home. But they both felt sure she had been holding something back and had probably been lying about much of the rest. And what about the missing forty-eight minutes between the time she said she had found the boy unconscious and the time she had run into the emergency room with him dead in her arms? And what about her unemotional behavior? They had talked to her about her son, who had been dead less than two days, and about her five other dead children, and she hadn't shed a single tear.

Pierce asked what her motive could have been, but neither man had a good answer. People who knew her said she'd been a good mother to the child, and the autopsy showed no signs of previous abuse. Hawkins had discovered that she had a $5,000 life insurance policy on the child and that there would be $2,225 left after the burial expenses were paid. But it seemed highly unlikely that any mother would murder her young son for such a small sum.

Pierce finally nodded his agreement; it was time for a search warrant. He picked up the phone and made several calls before locating Judge Paul Handy. Pierce handed the documents back to the detectives and watched as they rushed out of his office en route to getting the judge's signature. Pierce had held his elected office as Finney County attorney just slightly more than a year, and this was his first murder case. He could feel his stomach start to churn as he realized what probably lay ahead.

The detectives found Judge Handy, then took the signed warrant and raced to Diana's apartment. No one was there. They reasoned that since it was the day of José's burial, she and her family were probably staying at her sister's house. And they didn't want to break down the door to the home of a woman who had just buried her child. They saw no other choice but to wait until the following morning.

Elliott spent another two hours at home that evening working at his computer—writing and rewriting his police reports until they were all perfect. Then he crawled into bed and spent a restless night wrestling with the one thought that kept intruding again and again. What if Diana was a killer and had already grabbed her things and fled?

When Elliott arrived at the LEC the next morning, his anxiety was barely under control. Seeing that Hawkins was not yet there, he picked up the phone and dialed Diana's apartment. He was hoping to allay his nagging fear that she had fled and to get her to come in to answer a few more questions— questions that would provide the additional evidence needed to obtain her arrest warrant. No one answered the phone.

In a near panic he jumped into his car and raced out to her apartment, where he found her car parked. He knocked loudly several times before she answered, and when she opened the door, he could see that he had awakened her. He apologized and asked her if she would come down to the Law Enforcement Center (LEC) and answer a few more questions. To his relief she said she would meet him there in an hour.

The LEC is a new multistory concrete building located a block from the Finney County Courthouse. It houses the Finney County Sheriff's Department, the sheriff's jail facilities, and the Garden City Police Department. A small courtroom occupies one half of the basement level.

It was a few minutes past noon when Diana walked into the lobby of the LEC in the company of her boyfriend, Thomas. After Elliott was called, he came out and led Diana upstairs to an interrogation room on the second floor. The room contained a metal table and three stiff-backed metal chairs. A one-way mirror lined the wall next to the door, and a tape recorder and telephone were on the table. There were no ashtrays; none of the Garden City detectives smoked.

Hawkins joined them, then Elliott activated the recorder and said, "This is Saturday, May 5, 1990. It's 12:15 P.M., and this interview is taking place at the Garden City Police Department in the interview room in the Investigative Section. Present in the room is myself, Detective Ken Elliott, Detective James Hawkins, and Diana Lumbrera."

Over the next three hours the two detectives had Diana tell and retell her version of the events of April 30 and May 1. They wanted to know more about her friends, her family, and her past. They wanted specifics about the deaths of her other five children. About halfway through the interview Ricklin Pierce showed up, so the detectives took a break and brought him up to speed. When the interview resumed, they left the door ajar so that he could sit outside and listen.

Overall, Diana did very poorly. She frequently contradicted her earlier versions of the events, and she would add new details each time to make her stories more believable. She did give the detectives an extremely valuable piece of information, however. She confirmed finding José unconscious at nine o'clock, because her TV soap opera, *Simply Maria*, had just ended. That fact proved that she had waited at least forty minutes before going for help.

After three hours Diana was tired, and so were the detectives. The two men felt they had heard enough, so Elliott looked Diana square in the eye and said, "Okay, Diana, we've had our discussion, and some of the pieces don't fit together here. And I think you've told us a lot of information, but I don't think you've told us everything. Okay?"

"Well, a lot had gone on—"

"And, yeah, I know a lot's gone on," Elliott continued. "What I want to do is to protect us all. I want to ask you some more questions, but before I do that, I want to go ahead and read you your rights, your constitutional rights. Okay?"

Diana stared at him, her eyes wide with fear, as he calmly continued. "Here's why," he said. "It's going to protect us, because some of the things I want to ask you could be incriminating, okay? And you'll understand here once I read your rights to you. . . ."

"I don't understand," she pleaded, looking from one detective to the other. "What are you trying to tell me—that you're reading me my rights 'cause you're gonna arrest me?"

"Well, what I'm telling you is that it is a possibility, okay?"

"But I've done nothing!" she screamed.

"All right," responded Elliott, bringing his palms up as if to deflect her anger, "but before I can ask you these questions, we have to follow formalities, and one of them is this."

With that he pulled out a Miranda sheet and read her those rights. Then he asked if she was willing to speak with them without an attorney being present.

Her answer came quickly through clenched teeth. "No! I think I should get me a lawyer. I'm getting a lawyer, because I don't want you accusing me of things I didn't do, 'cause I tried everything I could do for my son."

The interview was over; Diana had invoked her constitutional rights. She demanded to use the phone to call her attorney, so Hawkins pushed the telephone in front of her. A few minutes later she stormed out of the room.

Hawkins looked over at Elliott and said flatly, "She's guilty."

Chapter 5

In Detective Hawkins's words, "the cat was out of the bag," so they had to act fast before Diana could return home and destroy whatever evidence remained. Elliott quickly assembled a search team comprising himself, Captain Armentrout, undercover narcotics investigator Michael Utz, and uniformed patrol sergeant Edwin Knight. Pierce and Hawkins would meet them at Diana's apartment later.

Elliott and Utz jumped into an unmarked car and hurried to Diana's apartment. Diana's car was already parked in front of the duplex. As they hurried toward the door, Thomas suddenly walked out with a partially filled plastic trash bag under his arm. The two detectives identified themselves and escorted him back into the apartment to search the bag. They found nothing incriminating in it.

Diana was in her bedroom, sitting on the waterbed and talking on the telephone. Utz walked in, identified himself, and asked her to hang up. She began to argue with him, so he grabbed the receiver from her hand and slammed it down. He had been working the streets a long time, and he no longer had patience for suspects who refused to listen.

Elliott had been watching from the living room. Now he walked in and explained that they were serving her with a legal search warrant. Diana was stunned. She knew that they suspected her of killing José, but she had not expected them to come and search through her things so soon. She was both frightened and angry, and she stood off to one side and watched. Minutes later Armentrout and Knight arrived to help.

Pierce and Hawkins had stayed at the LEC to work on the arrest warrant. Once it was ready, they went in search of the "on call" judge, and fifteen minutes later the warrant was signed. Hawkins relayed that fact to Elliott by radio.

Elliott acknowledged Hawkins's message, then turned to Diana and said, "Diana Lumbrera, you're under arrest for the murder of your son, José Antonio Lumbrera." Her reaction was one of shock. She stood motionless, unable to say anything, while Utz stepped forward and snapped handcuffs on her wrists.

Sergeant Knight took her by the elbow and was leading her toward the front door when she began to cry. "Why are you doing this to me?" she pleaded. But no one answered. Knight walked her outside, put her in the patrol car, then drove her straight to the jail. A few minutes later Piece and Hawkins arrived at the apartment.

The search warrant Elliott carried specified that the detectives could look for and confiscate any papers, ledgers, diaries, bank statements, bills, written correspondence, canceled checks, bank deposit slips, memorandums, notes, and letters. These items would help them to verify whether or not Diana had been in desperate need of money.

The list of papers would also allow them to impound any documentation of insurance policies on José and on Diana's other dead children, along with their death certificates. They wanted to know if the others had been insured and what had been given as the official cause of death for each child.

The warrant also mentioned bedding. During their initial interview with Diana, she had given them permission to take the sheets and pillow slips that she said had been on the waterbed at the time of José's death. Those items had already been sent to a lab in Topeka to be checked for traces of vomit. The results of those tests would later show that no traces had been found. Now the detectives wanted the legal right to confiscate any other waterbed bedding found so that it could also be checked.

Lastly, the warrant included any medications and prescription drugs that had José's name on them. His medical records showed that on the night of April 30, the doctor at the hospital had given Diana four vials of amoxicillin, an antibiotic, and directed her to give one to José that night, then to give him the remaining three the following day. Diana had repeatedly said that she had done so. But the detectives thought that if Diana had planned on killing José, she might not have bothered.

The officers made some interesting discoveries. The first was a pile of overdue bills. It included notes from a collection agency in Wichita, past due notices from Wesley Medical Center, a nonpayment notice from an insurance company, a notice of overdue note from a credit bureau in Wichita, a notice demanding payment from a credit bureau in Garden City, a past due notice from Furniture Warehouse in Garden City, a notice of delinquent payments from a credit bureau in Montana, a letter from an attorney regarding her overdue account with the cable company in Garden City, and several notices from the Ford Motor Credit Corporation requesting overdue payments for her compact car. Diana clearly had serious money trouble.

They also found a small plastic bag in the refrigerator that contained three vials of amoxicillin. None of the vials had been opened. No other bedding that would fit the waterbed was found.

Then they made a gruesome discovery. While searching a drawer, one of the men came across some photographs. One was of a young girl lying in an open casket; it was the only picture of Diana's other five dead children that they would find. And with it were some of her children's newspaper death notices, which had been laminated in plastic. These were strange remembrances for a mother to keep.

The detectives wanted to impound these items as evidence, but since photographs hadn't been included in the warrant, one of them had to leave to obtain a second search warrant while the others continued to dig.

Pierce decided to walk around the apartment to get a better sense of what kind of person Diana Lumbrera really was. What struck him about the home was that although it was neat and clean, there was something very strange about it—it was devoid of any sign of the child's presence. Parents of young children always have toys or clothes or special mementos of their children scattered around their home. But except for two framed photographs of the boy, there was nothing visible to suggest that the child had ever existed—and he had been dead less than four days.

Pierce picked up the photos and studied them. It was the first time he had seen the four-year-old boy, and seeing his picture finally made him seem real. José Antonio Lumbrera had been an attractive child with big brown eyes and a beautiful smile. How could anyone possibly murder this little boy? Pierce asked himself. Just thinking about it made him feel sick.

He handed the photographs to one of the detectives to be marked as evidence, then walked through the rest of the apartment. He wasn't surprised to see that Diana Lumbrera was very self-absorbed. Her apartment had two bedrooms, and she had taken one all for herself. She had obviously spent a lot of time and money decorating her bedroom with nice furniture and other things she liked, including a number of large stuffed teddy bears—some still in plastic bags. She had given very little thought to her son's needs, however. José shared the other bedroom with the roommate, Marguerite. And, except for two old beds and an old wooden chest, that room was completely empty. Even the walls were nearly bare. Utz finally found the child's toys in a closet in the front hallway. They were a sorry collection: an old tricycle with one wheel missing, a toy gun, and a couple of other small items that were broken. Pierce became depressed just looking at them.

At one point it occurred to him that Diana might have used one of those big plastic bags that had covered the stuffed animals to suffocate the boy, so he had the detectives search for a bag. They even looked in the dumpster outside the apartment, but found nothing. Each of the men had his own ideas about how the child had been killed.

The detectives were just finishing their search when the victim's godmother, Christina Hernandez, stopped by the apartment. She was a small, neatly dressed woman whose eyes were red and swollen from crying. She had come to comfort Diana and was shocked to learn that these men thought Diana had killed José.

One other visitor dropped by the apartment before the detectives left: Diana's younger sister, Isabel. She became instantly belligerent when told that Diana had been arrested for the boy's death. She said Diana could never have killed her own children and asked Hawkins if he had ever heard of witchcraft. When he said yes, she explained that someone in Diana's past had put a curse on her and that it was this curse that had caused the deaths of Diana's children.

Hawkins, who had once lived in Mexico for a year while attending a university there, was well aware of the strong beliefs that many in the Hispanic culture held about the powers of black magic. And in the past few days he had wondered more than once about what Diana's large, close family thought about the deaths of all her children. Had she really convinced them that someone's curse had been responsible?

Soon the second warrant was delivered, and when the evidence from that search had been collected and tagged, Elliott, Utz, and Pierce drove back to the LEC together. En route, Elliott received a radio call from the police dispatcher—Diana Lumbrera had asked to speak to him. He thought that Diana had probably decided to confess, so as soon as they arrived at the LEC, he and Utz hurried upstairs to the jail to talk to her.

Elliott and Utz escorted Diana from the jail section to the same small interview room they had used before. She had already been booked and was dressed in the standard issue, a bright orange cotton jumpsuit with the word "jail" stenciled in large black letters on the back.

Diana had asked for this interview because she hadn't been able to reach her lawyer and panic had set in. But her intent was not to confess. She apparently thought that she would be able to convince these men of her innocence if she had another opportunity to explain José's death.

Elliott again advised her of her rights and gave her an opportunity to call her attorney. When she still couldn't reach the man, she told the two detectives she wanted to talk to them anyway, then signed a waiver of her rights. The third interview began.

Diana's fear was obvious as she went over the same old story. Elliott didn't want to hear it again, and he had to force himself to sit quietly and wait until his partner, a highly skilled interrogator, found the perfect opening.

"Let me ask you this," Utz finally said. "Were you the only person in your apartment with José on the night that he died? Could someone else have broken in without your knowing it?"

"No, I was there by myself, and no one broke in."

"Then, if you were the only one in the apartment, only you could have smothered José."

The detective's logic caught Diana off guard. She looked down, trying to think, then finally nodded her head.

But a nod of the head wasn't enough. Utz wanted a clear confession from Diana. He knew that she was now vulnerable, so he leaned forward, stared her straight in the eye, and said, "Diana, it's not a question of *if* you suffocated your son, José, but *why* you suffocated him."

"But I've done nothing!"

"Diana, I just want to find out *why* you would have done something like this to José." This was a lead-in to an effective interrogation technique. If Diana was guilty and he presented her with an "out" for her actions, she would probably take it. "I want to believe that it was an accident or that you just didn't know what you were doing when you suffocated José with the pillow."

"It wasn't a pillow."

"That's just an example," Elliott quickly interjected to keep her on track.

"Diana, have you ever had black-out spells where you've been standing in one place and then minutes later you couldn't recall what you just did?"

"Yeah! About two months ago when I was taking a break at work—I was standing and writing on a pad of paper, and a few minutes later I found myself standing there and realized that I had blacked out. I couldn't remember what I'd just done."

He asked her if she had gotten any medical treatment for that blackout, to which Diana sadly replied, "No."

"Well, Diana, what we want to believe is that you blacked out moments before you found your son not breathing, and that you suffocated him during that spell, and that after the spell you found yourself standing over him and discovered that he wasn't breathing, but you didn't realize what you had just done. Diana, I want to believe that this was what happened and not that you had planned to do it for financial gain—because we know about the life insurance policy you had on José."

"I didn't intentionally do anything!"

"Well, do you think you blacked out and suffocated your son, then afterward found yourself standing over him and discovered that he wasn't breathing?"

Diana paused for a few seconds, then looked down and said softly, "Yeah, that's probably what happened."

The detectives had a few last questions. They wanted to know if she had taken any drugs or drunk any liquor before her son's death. The implication was that maybe drugs or booze had caused the blackout. But Diana denied having taken anything. She wanted to make it clear that she had been a victim of the blackout and that she had not caused it herself.

The interview then ended. It had taken less than one hour, and while the detectives hadn't yet secured a complete confession, they hoped that it, along with the other evidence they were collecting, would be enough to convince Diana to tell them the whole truth soon. Elliott returned to his desk and telephoned Pierce. The attorney was relieved when he heard the results.

But when Diana returned to her cell, she reflected on the things she had just said and became even more frightened. She knew she had said too much and swore she would not be tricked again. She had no intention of assuming any responsibility for the death of her son.

When Hawkins arrived at work Monday morning, he found a report on his desk that had been written by Jean Beld, a female jailer who had been supervising Diana Lumbrera for the past two nights. The report described a conversation the two had had in which Diana had talked of black magic.

In her report Ms. Beld wrote: "[Diana] wanted to know if it was all right if she made a long-distance phone call to Mexico and talk to a Sister Teresa. I asked her if she's a voodoo doctor. She said, 'Yes.' . . .

"She told Sister Teresa that she had tried to convince the police that she [had] not hurt her child, nor [had] she killed him. She explained to the person on the phone that she had seen witches and bats and [heard] noises in the house and [she talked] of the curse that had been placed on her. She asked the person on the phone to please help her. She then hung up the phone."

Hawkins's curiosity was piqued. He immediately walked upstairs to the jail section and was delighted when Diana agreed to talk to him.

He took her into an interview room and listened as she spoke to him in secretive whispers. She explained that she had actually seen a *lechuza*, a vicious, predatory owl-type bird that is associated with witches and that is believed to have the ability to change into human form. She explained that in the past few weeks she had been hearing owls whistling outside her home and had even seen several.

She said that about three weeks before the death of her son, she had seen a large black *brujo*, a male witch with red eyes and black wings, sitting in the small tree outside the kitchen window of her apartment. She had also been hearing unusual sounds in her home and had even heard footsteps at night but had never seen anyone there. She had heard the owls whistling and heard what sounded like scissors in the night and was convinced that someone had cast an evil spell on her.

She said that when she was lying in her jail cell the night before, she had even heard a very scary voice that said, "You are next." She understood what it meant; now that her son was dead, she would be the next to die.

Hawkins asked her if the voice had been male or female, and she answered that she had not been able to determine that. However, it had been a very eerie voice.

Diana want on to explain that very odd things had been happening to her recently and that she felt they had all been signs that someone had cast an evil spell on her. For example, every afternoon before leaving for work, she had turned on the porch light, but every night when she returned home, the light was always burned out.

She said she believed that her son had also heard the voices and the noises. One night there was a noise outside, and her son became frightened and asked her if it was *el coco* (the boogeyman). She told him that it was nothing, but she actually thought it was another owl.

Hawkins said nothing, but the tragic irony of Diana's last words struck him deeply. He knew the innocent child had had no way of knowing that *el coco* was his own mother.

Diana said she also believed that her son had had a premonition that something bad was going to happen on the day that he died, because he was unusually affectionate. He hugged her frequently and kissed her often, and he kept saying, "I love you, Mama." She had answered him by saying that she loved him too.

"Diana, had you seen and heard these same things just before your other children died?" asked the detective.

She said she had seen and heard the phantoms before the death of one of her other children. All the others had died in hospitals, and she had not seen any demons during those times. She blamed the person who had cast the spell on her for the deaths of her children and her mother. She said everyone thought that her mother had died of cancer, but she knew that her mother had also been killed by the evil spell.

"Well, do you think it might be possible that whoever cast an evil spell on you could have caused *you* to kill your children?" asked Hawkins, employing the same interrogation strategy as Utz had.

Diana wasn't going to be tricked twice. She said she didn't know. *Brujos* were very powerful and could probably do anything they wanted. If a person knew that someone had caused a spell to be cast on them, however, she could counteract that spell by getting another witch to break it, or she could break it herself by doing repetitive spell-breaking incantations. Diana said her mother had told her these things, but she didn't actually know how to do them herself.

That was as much as Diana wanted to say about witchcraft, but there was one other point she wanted to make. The detectives with whom she had spoken on Saturday afternoon had said something about an insurance policy that she had on José. She wanted Hawkins to know that it was true that she had a lot of debts but she loved her son very much and she would not have killed him for the money.

When Hawkins returned to his office he sat down in his chair, pulled a report form out of his desk, then paused before writing up the interview. He had met a lot of people, but he had never met anyone like Diana Lumbrera. She was a pretty woman who could tell a convincing story, but he could feel a kind of evil in her that frightened him. He hoped Ricklin Pierce would put her in prison for a very long time.

Chapter 6

In the afternoon edition of the *Garden City Telegram*, large, bold headlines on the front page announced: "Mother Arrested for Son's Murder." Underneath was a large photo of the duplex on Tonio Street. The reporter assigned to the story had contacted the chief of police in Bovina, Texas, for information about Diana's past, so the story mentioned that Diana had had five other children who had died. But the Bovina police chief felt strongly that the deaths had been from natural causes. He said that after being contacted recently by other police authorities, he had looked at the reports from autopsies performed on two of Diana's children. "There was nothing in the autopsies that appeared suspicious. Nothing at all. I wasn't here then, but I've looked at the [reports from] two autopsies and talked to several people about the deaths that occurred here, and there wasn't anything suspicious about any of the deaths at the time they happened. And I haven't found anything in the two autopsies that would indicate anything different."

He went on to describe the reaction of one of Diana's sisters. "She's real upset. She just doesn't believe there's any way her sister could do that to her children. [Diana's] family here is very law-abiding, very truthful and straightforward. They're well thought of around town."

The reporter also interviewed Diana's landlord in Garden City, a man who obviously respected Diana and who had been very fond of little José. "She's a good tenant," he said. "Like a lot of single parents, she's had a tough time once or twice, but she always did what she said she would do. Whenever we were over working at the house, [José] was always there. He was an active little guy. He was always around. I thought maybe he just wanted to hang around the guys a little bit."

The landlord went on to say, "I just hope there's nothing to it. As far as my experience with her, she's a real decent person." It was an opinion that the landlord would keep during the entire police investigation, one that would cause him to withhold important information from the investigators.

In fact, even Captain Armentrout had trouble believing Diana had killed her son. He had met her once months earlier when she was having problems with a rowdy neighbor. He remembered thinking that she was a very neat, polite, and reserved woman and that her little boy was real cute. He had questioned the landlord at the time, and the man had spoken very highly of her. It wasn't until the day of

Diana's arrest that Armentrout realized that she was the same woman.

On Tuesday, another story about Diana's arrest ran in the *Garden City Telegram*. It showed a large picture of Diana sitting in the courtroom, her hands held up in a praying position, her pretty face the pitiful picture of a distraught mother; she was the victim of a system gone wrong.

The headline read, "Mother Weeps at Murder Charge." As did the earlier story, this one hinted that Diana was the victim of an unjustified prosecution. It quoted Diana's sister, Isabel, who lived in Garden City.

Isabel described the deaths of two of Diana's other children and explained how they had died despite Diana's valiant attempts to save them. She said that most of their family had come to Garden City for Jose's funeral, then had left on Saturday to return to Texas. "And thirty minutes after everyone is gone," she said, "the police go and arrest her for murder."

Pierce was in his office when the secretary brought in the office copy of the newspaper. He picked up the paper, read the Lumbrera article, then threw it on the floor. The article made him angry, and he worried that it might bias public opinion against his case. Only 25,000 people lived in Garden City, and such a bias would make finding a fair jury very difficult, maybe impossible. He wondered why the reporter seemed so intent on painting Diana as the victim.

He tried to refocus his attention on his work.

Before the interruption he had been in the second hour of rereading all the Lumbrera case reports, then inserting them chronologically into an oversized three-ring binder. Those reports would serve as the basis for his trial notebooks.

He picked up the next report and started to read, but the news article was still worrying him. He pushed his chair away from the desk and stretched. Then he put his feet up, relaxed back into the leather chair, and thought about the police reports he had just read. It still amazed him to think that a mother would murder her child for money. And how about her other five children, who had died in Texas? Diana Lumbrera wasn't stupid, but she wasn't clever either. So if she had also killed those children, why hadn't she been caught?

He had no answer for that question, but he knew that she wouldn't go unpunished for José's murder. Only a week had passed since the child's death, and he almost had enough evidence to convict her. And even though Kansas didn't have the death penalty, a conviction for first-degree murder would put Diana in prison for at least fifteen years.

He swung his legs down, pushed himself up from the chair, and walked to the large window that overlooked the side lawn of the old courthouse. "No, there's nothing to worry about here," he reassured himself. "This one's in the bag."

He had no idea that before two weeks passed, his entire case would start to unravel.

PART II

THE TEXAS INVESTIGATION

Chapter 7

Deputy Richard Bonham pulled his patrol car slowly up to the intersection, turned north onto Highway 60, and headed for the nearby farm town of Friona. He loved living in the Texas Panhandle—the vast open plains, the endless blue sky, the clean, dry air. The traffic was light, as was usual in this sparsely populated area, so he figured it would take him twenty-five minutes to reach the funeral parlor.

Three days earlier Captain Armentrout had telephoned the Parmer County sheriff's deputy and asked for help in finding information on a Diana Lumbrera, AKA Diana Garza, and her five dead children. She was a strong suspect in the death of her last child, which had occurred in Kansas.

Bonham's entire department comprised one sheriff, four deputies, and a few civilian personnel. And since he was the one who had taken Armentrout's call, he had gotten the assignment. He was a man who enjoyed life and enjoyed a good laugh, but he could find no reason for laughter in the matter at hand. He was a single parent who was raising his twelve-year-old son alone, and he found the thought that a mother might have murdered her child more than a little chilling.

He had already checked the Parmer County clerk's office and found some of the needed documents. There were birth certificates for Diana's four children who had been born in Parmer County and death certificates for the three who had died there.

After a little more digging, he located two marriage certificates issued to Diana Lumbrera. One was for a marriage to a Mario Jaramillo on December 24, 1972, when Diana was only fourteen years old. The other was for a marriage to a Tony Garza on February 2, 1977, when she was nineteen. He had also found a death certificate for Garza, who was apparently the father of Diana's first four children.

The clerk had made two sets of photocopies of those records for him, and he had already mailed one set to Captain Armentrout. But there was still a lot to learn.

Bonham needed to know where her other child had been born and where her other two children had died. That information would show him where to look for their official documents. He needed to know which hospital she had taken the children to and whether autopsies had been performed on any of them. He also needed to know what kind of a person Diana was, where she had lived, the circumstances surrounding the deaths of each child, et cetera.

He had called John Blackwell, the owner of the only funeral home in Parmer County, Ellis-Blackwell Funeral Home, and arranged to pick up copies of his records on the children's burials. Then he obtained the necessary subpoena and headed for Friona. He hoped those records would provide some of the answers he needed.

Half an hour later, Bonham reached Friona and turned left onto Main Street. Like all the other towns in this part of the Panhandle, Friona was a town in decay and had a population of fewer than four thousand. The funeral home was just a few blocks up the street.

Bonham pulled the car into the adjacent parking lot. The building was an aging converted residence sandwiched between commercial buildings, which were now vacant. Its interior was decorated with a respectable blend of soft, neutral colors, thick carpets, and old, elegant draperies. There were no flowers in sight, but as soon as Bonham entered, he could smell their sweet, lingering fragrances.

He looked around and, seeing no one, walked through the building until he found John Blackwell at work in a small, cramped office in the back. Blackwell was a short, friendly man in his mid-forties with a strong, clear voice and intense blue eyes. Bonham handed him the subpoena and sat on the couch opposite his desk. Then he removed a pen and small notebook from his pocket, smoothed his wavy silver hair into place, and looked up.

"Why are ya looking into these deaths?" Blackwell asked in his soft West Texas drawl.

"Oh, they're part of a homicide investigation that's being conducted in Kansas. They think the mother might have murdered her last child, a little four-year-old boy."

"Well, I hope ya don't think those children were murdered," Blackwell said, shocked at the idea. "Those deaths were due to a genetic abnormality. That was proven years ago."

"Well, we're not so sure about that anymore—at least we're going to look into it now. Did you handle the funerals for these three children?"

"The only one that I personally handled was Melinda, who died in '82, and it was because of her that we learned about this genetic defect that was causing the children's deaths."

"What do you mean?"

"Well, as I recall, Melinda died sometime very early in the morning, and they called us shortly afterward, so we went to the hospital within an hour or so after that. It was while we were there that the nursing staff told us that she was the third or fourth child the mother had lost. They were suspicious of the child's death, so they had already called the justice of the peace, and she had already ordered an autopsy.

"Well, look, I'm from a law enforcement family," continued the funeral director, "plus I'm a reserve deputy sheriff, so I'm naturally kind of suspicious. And when I heard that, I immediately got *real* suspicious, ya know?

"I called Bruce Purdy in Muleshoe, the child's doctor, who was also a friend of mine, and he said he believed the woman was killing her kids. I had to agree with him. Their deaths just didn't make any sense. Then I called the sheriff, who was a good friend of mine, and I told him that with this many kids dying, there had to be something very wrong going on and that I thought that he ought to look into their deaths.

"Afterward I personally took the child to a funeral home in Amarillo and met with the pathologist there and told him about the other three Garza children who had died. Then I stayed and watched while he performed the autopsy."

"Who was that pathologist?"

"His name was Erdmann, Dr. Ralph Erdmann," explained Blackwell. "He was a forensic pathologist who was doing Amarillo's autopsies at the time, and later on he contracted with a number of counties, including ours, so he was eventually doing all of our autopsies."

"So, where did Erdmann perform the girl's autopsy?"

"Well, he met me at Boxwell's Funeral Home in Amarillo and did the autopsy there."

"And you stayed and watched?"

"Right. I stayed right there and watched. And he started showing me things," Blackwell explained, using his hands to illustrate how the pathologist had held up the heart while pointing out its flaws.

"And, of course, I've been around a lot," he continued, "but I'm not a physician—but anyway, he removed the heart and started pointing out things on it and telling me, 'Right here shows where she had this congenital heart defect, and right here shows—blah, blah, blah.' He said, 'This child had to have had a serious heart murmur.' And he said, 'She never would have lived.' " The funeral director had clearly been convinced.

"Did he do a complete autopsy?"

"Well, I don't really remember how much further he looked. Dr. Erdmann is the kind of man that once he finds what he's looking for, he doesn't bother to look anywhere else, ya know, which helps us as funeral directors, because a cranial is so much harder to cover up and what have ya, that we're always tickled to death when he doesn't do a cranial, because it means less work for us."

The deputy thought this was a revealing bit of information, and it made him a little nervous. He made a notation in his notebook, then asked, "How long do you think that autopsy took?"

"Oh, not long," Blackwell said, untroubled by his knowledge of Erdmann's faulty autopsy procedures. "You know, at the time our youngest daughter had had a heart murmur for years, and we had always been concerned about it. We had even taken her to a number of doctors, and they had all told us that it was a functional murmur, so there was nothing to worry about.

"Well, Erdmann got me so scared telling me how only pediatric cardiologists could recognize a serious heart murmur that, as soon as we could, my wife and I took our daughter to a pediatric cardiologist. And he told us that she did have a serious problem with her heart and that we should watch her very carefully. Ya see?" Blackwell said with conviction. "Erdmann was right!"

"How's your daughter today?"

"Oh, she's fine. Never did have any trouble with that murmur. Anyway, I came back from Amarillo feeling very guilty for even thinking that the child's poor ol' mama had killed her baby, ya know." The funeral director still felt bad for having had such thoughts.

"It made me wonder why she just didn't get herself fixed," he continued, "so that she wouldn't keep putting her children and herself through all that grief. Ya know, she had another one die a few years later in Dimmitt, a little boy, I think. That poor mother . . .

"Well, as soon as I got back to my office, I called Bruce Purdy, the child's doctor in Muleshoe, and told him what Erdmann had said, and he got real angry. He said, 'This child *never* had a murmur! This child was in perfect health!' and he said, 'I don't know where he's coming off on all of this, but—' Well, he just was convinced that the child had been murdered, but the autopsy proved that the death had been natural, you understand? And, of course, that meant there wasn't any need for the sheriff to do an investigation."

"I see. So when did the child's mother come to see you about the funeral arrangements?"

"Well, that's been so long ago, I couldn't tell ya. I'm going to guess that it was sometime in the early afternoon of that same day when they came in and made the funeral arrangements and everything."

"Do you remember her?"

"Oh, yes. I remember how emotional she was and how she'd faint, fall on the floor, and how everybody would gather around her and all this. Actually, I thought that was a little put on, ya know, but then I didn't really know her. Losing that many children, I would think that if anybody had a right to faint, she did."

"Did she have insurance on the child?"

"Yes, she had a thousand-dollar policy on the girl, I think. She assigned that money over to me to cover the funeral costs, but the costs were like three or four hundred dollars more than that, so we required her to go ahead and bring in the rest of the money, which she did."

"Do you know where she got that extra money?"

"No, I don't remember. I would imagine her family helped her out, because she had a big family, and they were real close."

"Where was the child buried?"

"At the Bovina Cemetery, where the others were buried. Of course, the mother only bought one lot at a time, so they all weren't buried alongside each other."

"Do you remember the service at the cemetery?"

"Well, not too much anymore. It's been a long time, but I do remember how she went on. In fact, I was told by the fellow that had been here before me, he said, 'Boy, you're in for something, because she really gets emotional, and she faints and all that,' so I'd already been cautioned about that before the service, and sure enough, she did."

"Was that the last time you saw the mother, at the burial?"

"Well, I might have seen her when she came in to pick up the death certificate, which she needed to give to the insurance company. I just don't remember. Oh, I did see her at her mother's funeral; we handled that one, too, and she carried on just the same. Actually, I think she kind of liked all the attention it brought her, but that's not to say that she didn't really feel bad about it all."

"Did she have insurance on the other children you handled?"

"Yes, she did, but I'm not sure about the face amount on their policies."

"How about autopsies on the others? Were any of them autopsied, too? Besides Melinda, I mean."

"Well, the mother had a little boy that died, the second one to die, I think. He got sick in Muleshoe and was transported to the Methodist Hospital in Lubbock. I owned the ambulance service in Muleshoe at the time, and we were the ones who transported him there. He died while he was still in the hospital, and I'm pretty sure an autopsy was done on him. "I don't know about the child that died in Dimmitt."

Bonham finished the notations in his notebook, the stood up and thanked Blackwell for his help. When he left, he was still suspicious of the children's deaths, and Blackwell was still convinced that the children had died from a congenital heart defect.

It would be another two years to the month before a major, unrelated scandal involving Dr. Ralph R. Erdmann would break wide open. An investigation into his autopsy procedures in five Texas counties would reveal inconsistencies in more than a hundred of his autopsy reports. Some of the bodies on which he had worked would even be exhumed, and an examination of those bodies would prove that his autopsies had been incomplete and his reports falsified.

Erdmann would enter into a generous plea bargain agreement with three of those five counties, arranged by district attorney Travis Ware of Lubbock County. Erdmann would plead no contest to several felony counts involving falsified autopsies, and in return he would receive a sentence of ten years' probation, several hundred hours of community service, and a requirement to pay only a fraction of the court costs. Erdmann would then surrender his license to practice medicine in Texas for five years and move to Washington state.

Chapter 8

Deputy Jerry Bailey hung up, took another swig of the cold, bitter coffee and thought about the name Diana Lumbrera. He was sure he had heard that name somewhere before. Bonham had just said that one of her children, a boy named Christopher, had died while she was living in Castro County, which was Bailey's jurisdiction, and Bonham needed a copy of the child's death certificate. Getting it would be no problem, but that would have to wait. Bailey had an idea he wanted to try first.

He jerked open the bottom drawer of the old wooden desk, dug through the pile of old files and books, then pulled out the local cross-reference directory for 1985. The book listed the names, addresses, phone numbers, occupations, and places of employment of all local residents of Dimmitt for that year. It was indexed by street address, last name, and phone number.

Bailey quickly found a listing for Diana Lumbrera. It showed that in 1985 she had worked at the Canterbury Villa, a local nursing home, and it listed her occupation as "nurse." It gave her address as a home in the 1200 block of NW Fourth Street in Dimmitt. Bailey knew that address; it belonged to David Salas, a lieutenant in a nearby police department.

Then he remembered. He had met Diana one day six years earlier at David's house. A relative of his, she was in her mid-twenties, a pretty, outgoing young woman dressed in skintight jeans and a revealing T-shirt. Bailey remembered that she had flirted a lot with some young men who had been there, but he didn't remember seeing a baby. She hadn't seemed the type who could kill a child, but then one never knew until something like that actually happened.

Bailey telephoned Salas and asked him to drop by the sheriff's office later that day. Then he went to the county clerk's office and picked up a copy of Christopher's death certificate.

Bailey, a large, good-natured family man in his early forties, was a deputy of the tiny Castro County Sheriff's Department, which was located in Dimmitt. As soon as Salas arrived, he led him to the small conference room at the back of the building and closed the door. He poured his friend a cup of coffee, offered him a cigarette, then sat down and relaxed. He tried to ignore the discomfort he was feeling with the questions he was about to ask.

Salas was a tall man in his late thirties, dressed in a dark blue police uniform that accentuated his good looks. Bailey began with some small talk, then finally got to the point.

"David, I need to talk to you about Diana, and I need you to tell me all you can about her, 'cause Kansas has her for the murder of her last child. They want to know about the other children."

Salas seemed surprised to hear of Diana's arrest, but he said nothing. He took a long drag off his cigarette, leaned back in the chair, and waited. He was no longer smiling.

"Now, I know there was another child of hers named Christopher," continued the deputy, "who died just shortly before I started working here. You remember his death?"

The lieutenant nodded his head and explained that she had given birth to the baby when she was living in New Mexico. She and the baby had moved in with him and his wife shortly afterward because they had no place to live. She soon got her own apartment, and it was there that the baby died. He admitted that the child's sudden death had surprised him.

He said he had been at work that day, and Diana had called him from the hospital and said that her boy was dead. He had gone straight there to be with her. When he arrived he found her standing in the hallway, and she said the baby had stopped breathing and that she had rushed it to the hospital but the doctors had failed to save it. She became very emotional and suddenly passed out. He grabbed her, carried her to a couch, then called his wife and told her to come take Diana back to their home. The lieutenant shrugged his shoulders to indicate that there was nothing more to tell.

Bailey asked for the names of Diana's brothers and sisters, which the lieutenant willingly provided. He also learned the name of Christopher's father, a man named Alberto Regas.

Bailey would later get a copy of the child's birth certificate, and on it a John Marcos would be listed as the baby's father. He already had a copy of the child's death certificate, and in the space provided for the name of the baby's father the word "unknown" had been written.

Salas pushed his chair away from the table and said with finality, "You know, you should talk to my mother. She knows more about it than me."

Bailey asked one last question. He wanted to know if his friend had ever been suspicious about the deaths of Diana's children?

Salas said there had been no reason for suspicion. There had been autopsies on the children, and they had all died from natural causes. He was finished talking, so he stubbed out his cigarette in the ashtray, stood up, and walked to the door. He hesitated for a moment in the doorway, then turned and gave the deputy some startling information.

He said that in 1980, three years before Christopher's death, Diana had taken a relative's baby girl to the hospital at Muleshoe, and the baby had been dead on arrival. An autopsy had been done, and he thought the cause of death had been listed as SIDS (sudden infant death syndrome). The child's name was Ericka Leonor Aleman, and she had been only six weeks old.

Bailey managed not to show how jolted he was by that last piece of information. He arranged to meet Ben Aleman, the father of that infant, later on that evening at the lieutenant's home.

After Salas left, Bailey grabbed the phone and called Deputy Richard Bonham in Farwell. He passed on the information he had obtained and told him about the meeting he would have that night.

Then he telephoned Detective James Hawkins in Garden City and asked for copies of all the reports generated in their case against Diana Lumbrera. Texas had officially begun its own investigation into the children's mysterious deaths.

Chapter 9

Bailey pulled the aging patrol car into the cement driveway of Salas's large ranch-style home and parked. He checked his watch to verify that he was on time, then hoisted himself out of the driver's seat, walked to the door, and knocked. A few seconds later the lieutenant was leading him down a hallway toward the rear of the house.

Most Hispanics who live in this part of Texas are Catholics and have large extended families whose members are very close. They are honest, hardworking, and law-abiding people who keep to themselves and rarely cause trouble. Often poorly educated, they find work as laborers on large grain and cattle farms or in the beef slaughterhouses and packinghouses. It's hard work, and it pays little, but it's often the best work they can get. The eldest male is considered head of the family, and in Ben Aleman's family it was Diana's father who played that role. That fact alone made Ben Aleman very nervous about talking to the deputy.

Salas led Bailey into the dining room where Ben, his mother, and his new wife were sitting around a large wooden table. Bailey could feel the tension in the air as he took his seat. Ben was a tall, heavyset man dressed in clean Levi's, a button-up work shirt, and black-rimmed glasses. He was a man who worked hard, lived an honest life, and had no trouble looking anyone in the eye. Bailey guessed that he was in his early forties.

The women served coffee, then sat down and listened in silence as the deputy asked his questions of Ben. First came the specifics—full name, date of birth, home address, et cetera. Then came the personal questions—the ones that made everyone uncomfortable.

Bailey learned that Ben and the baby's mother, Karen, had divorced about two years after the baby had suddenly died. Ben said that things had gone bad after the death. Then he paused for a moment and started at the beginning of his story.

Ben had been living in a worker's house on a large farm in Castro County with his wife, their eight-year-old daughter, Mary, and Casey, Karen's ten-year-old daughter from her first marriage. Ben wanted more children, so Karen became pregnant. It was during her pregnancy that Diana came by one day and told them that she and her little girl, Melinda, needed a place to stay. She was his cousin, so Ben and Karen agreed to let her and her child stay with them. In return, Diana agreed to help with the housework.

Everyone seemed to get along well, and a few

weeks later Karen gave birth to a healthy baby girl, Ericka. Karen had the doctor do a tubal ligation at the same time to make sure there would be no more children after this one. While recovering, Karen was very limited in what she could do, so Diana and the two older girls did nearly all of the cleaning and cooking. The baby was fine, except for a few infrequent bouts of colic.

The strain began to build in Ben's voice as his story reached the day little Ericka had died so suddenly.

On October 8, 1980, when Ericka was only six weeks old, Karen was feeling sick, so she stayed in bed that morning. Ben had been working in the fields near his home, and as was his habit, he returned home to check on his family at about ten o'clock. He remembered that the baby was healthy and happy at that time and that he played with her for a few minutes before returning to work. Half an hour later he saw Diana slowly pulling out of the driveway in his old car and heading toward Muleshoe. He had no idea where she was going.

Ben's voice grew angry, and his words became punctuated with profanity. He said when he returned home for lunch, he found his cousin, David Salas, and David's wife sitting at the kitchen table with Karen. David told him they needed to go to the hospital in Muleshoe immediately, because Diana had called from the hospital and said that baby Ericka was dead.

Ben couldn't believe it and asked what had happened. David told him what Diana had said, that when she was about twenty minutes from the house the baby let out a shriek. She stopped the car and noticed that the baby had stopped breathing, so she hit its chest with one hand to start it breathing again. It didn't work, so she held it in one arm and gave it mouth-to-mouth resuscitation while she raced it to the nearest hospital. She did her best, but the doctors weren't able to save it.

Ben became enraged. He knew his baby hadn't been sick, and even if she had, *he* would have been the one to take her to the hospital, not Diana. Karen knew that. He looked at Karen and demanded to know why she had let Diana drive off alone with their baby. Karen said Diana had told her that the baby was sick, then she had scooped the infant up in her arms and quickly left with her in Ben's car. Karen hadn't seen the baby herself, so she assumed Diana was telling her the truth.

Ben said he couldn't understand why his wife hadn't stopped Diana from taking the baby. Nor could he understand why Diana had left with his baby without telling him. Then as David drove them to the hospital, Ben thought about the sudden deaths of Diana's first three children, and a terrible feeling came over him.

As soon as they reached the hospital, he demanded that an autopsy be performed on the infant. The autopsy was performed the next day, but its results were inconclusive; the doctor wasn't able to find anything wrong with the infant that would have caused her death. That left Ben uncertain and confused. And without any proof that Diana had actually killed his child, he felt it better to say nothing.

Diana continued to live with Ben and Karen for another week or two, then she and Melinda moved out, and he never saw them again except at family gatherings.

Ben stopped and drank from his coffee cup, then said that Karen wouldn't even go to the baby's funeral, a fact for which he had never forgiven her. Things between them turned bad after that, and the marriage finally ended up in divorce. Now only bitterness remained. But he still wondered if his cousin Diana had murdered his baby.

More than an hour had passed when Bailey finally rose to his feet and thanked them all for their time. There was no hard evidence of murder in what he had just been told, but there certainly was reason for suspicion.

As he drove home he tried to guess what would cause a pretty young mother to murder her cousin's baby—and maybe her own as well. It made no sense to him. Bailey and his wife, Vicki, had two young children at home, and he loved being a father. He simply couldn't understand *why* anyone would do such an incredibly inhuman thing. Just the thought of it left him feeling sick and angry.

Chapter 10

Deputies Bailey and Bonham moved into high gear. Bonham collected documentation from the hospitals where the children had died, while Bailey searched out information about Diana's work and school history.

Bailey had already discovered that Diana had once worked at a nursing home, a fact which had created a eerie question in his mind. If Dana had killed young children, could she have also killed others who were equally as vulnerable? He soon learned that the nursing home that had once been Canterbury Villa had changed ownership years earlier, and all records from the period of Diana's employment had been destroyed.

He located one of Diana's former coworkers who remembered that she had worked there as a nurse's aide. She said she didn't remember anything unusual in the number of deaths that had occurred during Diana's employment—that is, anything unusual enough to arouse suspicion. And without records to check, it was a line of inquiry that would go nowhere. If any murders had been committed at the little nursing home, no one would ever know.

The Parmer County sheriff's office is housed in the old courthouse in downtown Farwell, a town so small that it has only one traffic light, and it blinks yellow twenty-four hours a day. Bailey agreed to meet Bonham there on Friday, May 11, so that they could share copies of everything they had found. They were using the copying machine in Bonham's crowded office when a call came through from Johnny Actkinson, the district attorney of Parmer County.

Actkinson, a balding, heavyset man in his early forties, told Bonham that the chief of police from nearby Bovina and a reporter from the *Garden City Telegram* in Kansas were in his office, and each had information on the Lumbrera children. He wanted the deputies to meet him and the two men in the district courtroom so they could go over all of the information that had been collected. This was Actkinson's first contact with the Lumbrera case.

Actkinson guessed that this task would prove to be a waste of time, because even though he knew very little about the case, he couldn't believe that any mother would murder seven helpless children. But he also knew that, on the outside chance that he was wrong, three or four of these cases would be his to prosecute. Therefore, he wanted the information in a format he could easily understand.

Fifteen minutes later, the five men were in the

district courtroom, arranging the information they possessed into organized stacks on the two large counsel tables. They worked for more than an hour, and when they were finished Actkinson had developed a list that provided the essential details of each case. It contained the following information, organized by the chronological order of death:

1. Born: Joanna Lumbrera
8/18/76

   Place: Friona, Parmer County, Texas

   Father: Tony Garza

   Died: Joanna Lumbrera
11/30/76

   Age: 3½ months

   Place: DOA Parmer County Community Hospital Friona, Parmer County, Texas

   Autopsy: No

   Cause of Death: Strangulation Due to Aspiration of Stomach Contents (Drowned in her own vomit)

2. Born: Luís Garza 11/28/77

   Place: Clovis, Curry County, New Mexico

   Father: Tony Garza

   Died: José Luís Garza
02/13/78

   Age: 2½ months

Place: Methodist Hospital
Lubbock, Lubbock
County, Texas

Autopsy: Yes

Cause of Death: Undetermined

3. Born: Melissa Lumbreros
03/14/75

Place: Bovina, Parmer
County, Texas

Father: Tony Garza

Died: Melissa Lumbrera
Garza 10/02/78

Age: 3 years, 6 months

Place: DOA Parmer County
Community Hospital
Friona, Parmer
County, Texas

Autopsy: Yes

Cause of Death: Asphyxia Due to
Aspiration of Stomach
Contents (Drowned in
her own vomit)

4. Born: Ericka Leonor Aleman
08/25/80

Place: Dimmitt, Castro
County, Texas

Parents: Ben and Karen Aleman

Died: Ericka Leonor Aleman
10/08/80

Age: 6 weeks

Place: DOA West Plains
Medical Hospital

		Muleshoe, Bailey County, Texas
	Autopsy:	Yes
	Cause of Death:	Undetermined
5.	Born:	Melinda Ann Garza 11/29/79
	Place:	Muleshoe, Bailey County, Texas
	Father:	Tony Garza
	Died:	Melinda Ann Garza, 08/17/82
	Age:	2 years, 9 months
	Place:	DOA Parmer County Community Hospital Friona, Parmer County, Texas
	Autopsy:	Yes
	Cause of Death:	Acute heart failure due to increased taxation on a case of congenital heart disease
6.	Born:	Daniel Christopher Marcos 10/10/83
	Place:	Clovis, Curry County, New Mexico
	Father:	John Marcos
	Died:	Christopher Daniel Lumbrera 03/28/84
	Age:	5 months
	Place:	DOA Plains Memorial Hospital

	Dimmitt, Castro County, Texas
Autopsy:	No
Cause of Death:	Septicemia (Blood infection)
7. Born:	José Antonio Lumbrera 02/21/86
Place:	Garden City, Finney County, Kansas
Father:	Juan Martinez
Died:	José Antonio Lumbrera 05/01/90
Age:	4 years, 3 months
Place:	DOA St. Catherine's Hospital Garden City, Finney County, Kansas
Autopsy:	Yes
Cause of Death:	Asphyxia due to smothering

It was an interesting and informative document, but it still didn't convince Johnny Actkinson that Diana had murdered any of the children. The Bovina police chief and the newspaper reporter agreed with Actkinson. Bailey and Bonham weren't so sure.

Five things struck the two deputies immediately.

First, of the four Texas autopsies that had been performed, two had listed "undetermined" as the cause of death. In addition, John Blackwell's description of Dr. Ralph Erdmann's autopsy of Melinda made it clear that Erdmann's findings couldn't be trusted; he hadn't performed a complete autopsy on the girl. That meant three of the four autopsies had "undetermined" findings, and that was certainly grounds for suspicion.

Second, although Diana had lived in the same basic area while in Texas, she had taken the dead children to three different hospitals. Why?

Third, of Diana's five children in Texas, three had been born under one name but buried under another. Again, why?

Fourth, even if a genetic agent had caused the death of Diana's six children, what about the death of Ericka Aleman? What were the odds that one woman would be present not only at the deaths of her six children but also at the death of a relative's infant?

And fifth, on all but two of the children's birth certificates, José Luís's and José Antonio's, Diana had omitted the previous births and deaths of her other children. Why had she tried to hide the fact that she had had other children who had died?

All of these questions led the deputies to ask the biggest question of all: if Diana had murdered six children in Texas, why hadn't she been caught before now?

As soon as Actkinson and the other two men left, the two deputies paid a visit to Dr. Bruce Purdy, the physician John Blackwell had mentioned. Dr. Purdy's office was located in a small clinic across from the only hospital in nearby Muleshoe. Purdy was a sensitive man of average height and build, with thinning salt-and-pepper hair, fair skin, and wire-rimmed glasses. He had been the family doctor for two of Diana's children, Melissa and Melinda. When he heard the reason for the deputies' visit, his eyes narrowed and his face reddened with anger.

"Well, it's been a long time, and I can't remember the exact time frames, but I can tell you this: Diana killed those kids! I knew she was doing it, but I couldn't get anybody to stop it!"

"When did you become suspicious?"

"Well, I became suspicious after the first death," he said. "She brought her baby into the emergency room with a little cold, and she ended up back in there three days later with the child. I wasn't on call when it happened, one of the other doctors was, but he told me that the baby came in dead. He said it was a pneumonia or something that I had missed, and I told him that was impossible. I knew that child wasn't really sick!

"Then she had one that ended up in Lubbock," he continued, "and I think she must have killed it over there while it was in the hospital. Allen Pace had also treated some of her children, so by that time we were both very suspicious. We discussed the matter many times, but we had no objective evidence to prove that their deaths weren't natural.

"It was when her third or fourth child died that I became convinced that she was killing those kids. I went straight to my office and called the Parmer County sheriff's office and talked to the sheriff himself. I told him point-blank, 'I know that she's killing those children, and I don't know what to do about it.' And he told me, 'We're keeping an eye on her. We know something's going on, and we're keeping an eye on her,' but nothing ever got done.

"Then they had some pathologist say that the death was from 'natural causes.' That was so ridiculous! I told 'em, 'I wish they'd let that woman babysit his kids, because—' Well," Dr. Purdy paused, his lips tight with anger.

"I remember that John Blackwell over at the funeral home was also suspicious, so he went up and watched that autopsy, then later he called me and said, 'Oh, it was congenital heart failure, and I feel so sorry,' like whatever that pathologist had said was etched in stone.

"And I said, 'John, give me a break! This isn't the first one that's died. Now, if it'd been the first one that had died, well, maybe. But not after two have already died.'

"I even called the Child Protective Services at the Texas Department of Human Resources, or whatever name it was called by at the time, and discussed my suspicions at length. They said, 'Okay, we'll send a caseworker out to investigate,' but as far as I know, they never did, so nothing ever happened. No one ever contacted me.

"The next time I saw her was when she came into my office again. She came in and told my receptionist that she wanted a pregnancy test, so my receptionist sent her down to the lab to be tested; it came back positive.

"Then she came back to my office, and my receptionist put her into a treatment room to wait for me. And when I walked in and saw her, I just couldn't believe it. I told her, 'I will not deliver your baby so that you can bring it back dead a few months later!' "

"How'd she react to that?" asked one of the deputies.

"She just acted indifferent, like she couldn't care less."

"What happened then?"

"Well, then I walked out and told my receptionist that Diana was pregnant but that we weren't going to be delivering that child. Then, several weeks later, Diana came into the hospital emergency room saying that she was having some problems with her pregnancy. She told them that I was her doctor, so they called me to go see her."

"Did you go?"

"You bet I did! I went straight down there and saw her. I even remember that she was over there in room number 34, and I walked in and told her, 'Diana, I am not going to deliver this baby and feel responsible for what you're going to do to it.' I told her right there, I said, 'I know what you're doing to those babies. Now, I can't prove it, but I know what you're doing. And don't you ever come in and see me again with this pregnancy!' I can tell you that I was *livid*!"

"What did she do then?"

"Nothing. She just looked at me with this little sneer of a smile on her face, like she enjoyed tormenting me, so I turned and walked out the door and slammed it behind me. That was the last time I saw her. I heard that that baby died in Dimmitt not long after it was born.

"Oh, I think she brought another dead child into the hospital over in Friona," the doctor suddenly remembered, "although I don't think that child belonged to her. It might have belonged to a relative of hers. I don't remember."

"Doctor, do you know if anyone else was present with those babies besides Diana when they died?"

"As far as I know, she was always alone with them when they died, at least with the ones I know about. The children supposedly stopped breathing at home and then she brought them to the hospital. See what I mean?"

The deputies saw exactly what the doctor meant. "Doctor, would you be willing to testify to these things in court," one of them asked, "that is, if this investigation gets that far?"

"I most certainly would! In fact, I'd look forward to it."

Bailey asked about getting copies of the children's medical records, and the doctor replied that he didn't know if any of the old records were still available but that he would check. Then Bonham instructed the doctor to write up his statement and mail it to him at the Parmer County Sheriff's

Office. At the end of that statement the doctor wrote:

"Thank God someone in Kansas finally had the courage to investigate and pursue what was obvious to many of us several years ago. I am dreadfully sorry for all the dead children that are not only her victims, but the victims of a liability-conscious society. No one ever had the courage to say, 'Lady, you can't keep killing your children.' "

The deputies wanted to interview Dr. Allen Pace, Dr. Purdy's colleague who had also treated Diana's children. However, Dr. Pace had moved his medical practice to Lubbock, the largest town in the Texas Panhandle, which was two hours southeast of Farwell. They returned to Bonham's office and telephoned him first.

This doctor was a cautious man, and he hesitated when he learned the reason for the visit they were planning to make. He said that he would have to consult his attorney before giving them a written statement.

He did confirm the statements that Dr. Purdy had made and agreed that he, too, had been very suspicious of the cause of the children's deaths. He said he had also refused to treat Diana or her children because her children always turned up dead later on.

And he gave them one lead. He suggested they contact a Dr. Kyle Mason in Clovis, New Mexico, because he had also treated one of Diana's children.

Dr. Pace said he might still have some of the family's old medical records, and he asked for a little time to locate them. He would provide them with copies if they would serve him with a subpoena.

The deputies thanked the doctor and told him that they would obtain the subpoena and serve it on him the following week.

Chapter 11

Two more weeks of digging into old records, running down possible leads, and talking to reluctant witnesses passed before the deputies decided to bring Texas Ranger Warren Yeager into the investigation. On Monday, May 21, the three men met for the first time in Bonham's small office.

Yeager was forty-two years old, ruggedly handsome in his standard ranger attire, and sounded like an old Texas cowboy when he spoke. His Old West image belied his status as a highly trained investigator who was very good at his job.

The deputies asked Yeager to investigate the Lubbock death of José Luís, Diana's second victim. They had two important reasons for doing so. First, Yeager worked out of the Lubbock office of the Texas Rangers, so it would be convenient for him to locate documents and talk to witnesses. And second, they had just learned that the Kansas case was in deep trouble, which meant they needed to get an indictment against Diana before Kansas was legally required to release her. There wasn't much time left.

The two deputies quickly brought Yeager up to date on what they and the Garden City investigators had learned so far, including the specifics about Diana Lumbrera's past. What they had pieced together provided some interesting insights into the woman's character.

Diana had been born in Friona, Texas, on November 21, 1958. Her father was a twenty-five-year-old laborer, and her mother was his nineteen-year-old wife. Diana was their firstborn, and she remained the favored child even though her mother gave birth to two more girls and four boys. Diana's parents gave her free rein over her younger siblings, and she ruled them with a heavy hand.

Diana had average intelligence, but she did poorly in school. Always big for her age, she was a bully with a quick temper who often picked fights with her classmates. She seemed to enjoy inflicting pain on others and would strike out with her fists or a rock or whatever was handy. With her teachers she was belligerent and would refuse to do her lessons. She had a special dislike for her male teachers and would constantly provoke them, then dare them to hit her. And although she earned failing grades, her teachers would still pass her up to the next level each year; giving her to someone else was easier than getting her to learn.

Diana hated school and missed classes whenever possible, using excuses such as headaches, backaches, and sore throats. She frequently complained of being "tired" and "not feeling well." Within the first two months of her eighth grade year, she had already been absent a total of two weeks. It was then, at the age of thirteen, that Diana apparently thought of a way to justify dropping out of school completely.

While at home one evening she told her parents that she was having burning pains in her head and chest and that she was dizzy. Then she "fainted" and began to have jerking movements on the left side of her body.

Her worried parents rushed her to the hospital in Friona, where she was kept for two days. They kept vigil at her bedside while doctors ran a series of tests to determine the cause of her symptoms. And even though those same jerking movements recurred in the presence of the doctors and nurses, nothing could be found to explain what was causing them. Nor could the doctors explain the reasons for the head and chest pains that Diana claimed she was experiencing. The doctors finally decided to transfer her to a larger, better equipped hospital in Amarillo where additional tests could be run.

The second hospital ran an extensive battery of tests on her, but still nothing could be found to explain her strange symptoms. The doctor wrote in Diana's medical file that she was "very theatrical and dramatic in her descriptions." He guessed that she was faking many of her symptoms.

During a conversation with her mother, the doctor learned that Diana had continually tried to avoid attending school and that she had been obsessed with the death of her grandfather, which had occurred more than a year earlier. Mrs. Lumbrera said that Diana frequently claimed to have seen her grandfather and to have talked to him since his death.

Diana's anxiety about attending school and her obsession with her grandfather's death were the only clues to her condition that the doctor could find. In his medical report under the heading "Mental Status Examination," he wrote, ". . . reveals an alert white female. Her speech is spontaneous, coherent and relevant. She does not seem to be overly endowed intellectually. She admits to feelings of nervousness. She had been worried over the death of this grandfather and states that she cannot seem to forget his death. . . ."

The doctor told Diana's parents that he thought her symptoms were psychosomatic, which meant conjured up in her mind, and had been brought on by her anxiety about her grandfather and about having to attend school. He suggested that they downplay her physical complaints and make her return to class. If they did otherwise, she would very likely establish a pattern with multiple recurring physical complaints. She was a hypochondriac in the making.

However, the doctor had already seen how Diana's family babied her when she allowed her leg and arm to jerk and how they carried on when she complained of burning pains in her head and chest. He didn't hold much hope for her recovery, in part because of her family members, and he made a note to that effect in his report.

He prescribed Valium for her and suggested that if the Valium didn't work, she should be taken for psychiatric treatment. During the remainder of her two-day stay in the hospital, the medical staff dispensed the drug to her along with their kind, sympathetic support. It was the kind of attention that Diana had always craved, and she obviously loved it. As she grew older she would look for ways to find that same kind of attention again and again.

Diana's hospital episode had been emotionally and financially draining for her family, so her parents had little objection when she said that she didn't want to return to school. They agreed that there would be less stress at home, therefore less chance for a repeat episode of the mysterious symptoms. And, with six younger children at home, Diana's full-time help there was very much needed.

But Diana had no intention of staying home to care for her younger siblings. She began dating neighborhood boys and staying out late at night. Only a few months passed before she came home one night and said she was leaving to marry an eighteen-year-old boy named Mario Jaramillo. She had just turned fourteen. Her parents objected because of her young age, but she left anyway. Diana wasn't one to take orders.

In the Hispanic culture it is the husband who is expected to earn the money and make all important decisions regarding his family. The wife is expected to keep his house, bear his children, and be obedient to his wishes. Mario and Diana moved into a little house in Bovina which was owned by a relative, then he quickly found full-time employment at a nearby grain mill. He was eager to fulfill his role as head of the family. But, not surprisingly, Diana flatly refused to be a compliant wife.

Apparently she didn't like staying home and doing housework, because she soon developed a reputation in the neighborhood as a girl who preferred having fun. She would dress up in skin-tight clothes and go out with her girlfriends to places where young men would congregate. She seemed to enjoy the sexual attention she got during those casual encounters. Some observers claim that Diana wanted more than admiring glances and that she sometimes left with her admirers and didn't return for hours.

Mario soon became disenchanted with his pretty young wife. He discovered that, in addition to her flirtatious behavior, she often lied to him and that she had a quick and violent temper when she didn't get her way. They battled constantly over money, Diana always demanding more than what he could give her.

He stayed with her for two years, hoping that her behavior would improve with time, but it didn't. It just got worse. One night, after one of her particularly violent episodes, he packed up his things and left. He had finally had enough.

The two-year marriage left Diana a changed person. To those around her she seemed more streetwise and determined to find ways to make quick money. And even though her disdain for men had obviously increased, she still wanted them—at least the ones she could control. She apparently wanted their money and their attention as long as she didn't have to give much in return.

When the deputies finished briefing the ranger, the three men discussed the six cases and what kind of evidence still needed to be found. They had accumulated a lot of information, much of it suspicious, but they didn't have the kind of clear, hard facts that a jury would understand and believe. Some of it wouldn't even be admissible in trial. What they needed were some good witnesses, credible people who had firsthand knowledge that Diana had lied about the circumstances of her children's death and who would testify to that fact at trial. The lawmen would have to dig deeper.

They were just wrapping up for the day when an unexpected phone call came through from a deputy of a sheriff's department in East Texas. The deputy said he had just received a telephone message from a man identifying himself as Tony Garza. Garza had read a story in his local newspaper about Diana Lumbrera's arrest in Kansas for the murder of her son. He explained that Diana was his ex-wife and that he wanted to tell the investigators about her and their four children who had died.

This news was surprising, because the lawmen had believed Garza to be dead. They had a copy of a death certificate with his name on it. They immediately sent a message for him to meet them at the sheriff's office in nearby Midland two days later.

At exactly one o'clock Tony Garza, his aging mother, and his two small children from his last marriage walked into the sheriff's office. His family took seats in the dusty little reception area, while he was ushered into the captain's office. Bailey, Bonham, and Yeager were already there waiting.

Garza was tall and stocky, with thick, wavy hair and a face that had once been unusually handsome. Now it bore the scars of a life that had seen far too much tragedy. He was employed as a fireman in a small town near the Oklahoma border.

He explained that his last wife and their other two children had died in a tornado several years earlier, so the three individuals who waited outside were all that remained of his family. Then, in a quiet voice, he began to talk about his days with Diana Lumbrera.

He said he had first met Diana in 1974, when he was living in a small town in New Mexico and she was living in Bovina, Texas. Diana had just turned sixteen, and he was a year older than she. She had been pretty and flirtatious, and they started dating soon afterward. A few months later, they moved in together but couldn't marry because she was still legally married to a boy named Mario Jaramillo. At Garza's insistence, she finally went to an attorney and filed for a divorce.

Garza said his relationship with Diana had been

stormy almost from the beginning. She had a violent temper, and on two different occasions she had attempted to run over him with their automobile during an argument. She had also chased him around the house with a butcher knife during one of her angry outbursts. Her violent behavior had surprised him, because she had always acted so nice when they were just dating. And besides, Hispanic women weren't supposed to act that way.

He said that Diana was, in fact, a very good actress. She constantly lied to him, even when she had no real reason to do so, and would often convince him of things that he would later discover weren't true. She sometimes used those things to humiliate him, especially when others were around. She was also a very jealous and vindictive person who would go to great lengths to hurt anyone who had made her angry. Looking back, he guessed that she had only stayed with him because he kept giving her money. Diana was like that; she used men to get what she wanted.

Their first child, Melissa, was born the first year they were together, when Diana was still sixteen. Being pregnant was a new experience for Diana, and she liked the way people treated her when they realized that she was an expectant mother. This was also her parents' first grandchild, and all the family lavished attention on Diana before and after the baby was born.

Melissa had been a pretty, healthy baby, and Garza felt that Diana had been a good mother to her. She had always seemed loving toward the child when he was around and had never abused her, at least as far as he knew. And she always did extra things—like buying her pretty dresses, having photos taken of her, and giving her birthday parties each year. He said Diana had been that way with all their children. She enjoyed the attention she got when people admired their kids.

He had hoped that Melissa's birth would improve their marriage, but it didn't turn out that way. Instead, Diana's rages became more frequent. She loved to party and began going out one or two nights a week with her girlfriends, while leaving him at home with the baby. He protested and refused to give her money, but that didn't stop her. She got the money somewhere else, but he was afraid to ask from whom or how.

Then, when Melissa was one and a half years old, their second child, Joanna, was born.

Being pregnant and giving birth was easy for Diana, but she didn't want a second child. It doubled her work at home and made it harder for her to go out partying—plus she didn't get as much attention with this second child as she had with her firstborn. Garza said that he and Diana had several big fights around that time, and one stood out vividly in his memory.

One evening he and Diana were arguing at the dinner table over money. He was working at a nearby beef packing plant, making a better wage than a lot of men older than he, but it was never enough money for Diana. She always wanted more. She became enraged and threw an iron skillet filled with hot oil at him, then screamed that she was going to kill Joanna and herself to get even with him for being such a lousy husband. In the weeks that ensued, she made similar threats during her frequent bouts of anger. He said he knew she was capable of terrible things, but he had never believed her capable of actually killing their baby or herself.

The lawmen could see from his expression that he was now having second thoughts. They wanted to know about the day Joanna died, November 30, 1976. Joanna was the first of the victims to die, and she was only three and a half months old at the time.

Garza's voice became softer, and sadness filled his eyes as he talked about that day. He said it was a normal workday for him, and he had gotten up early and dressed in his work clothes. Before leaving the house, he had gone into the girls' room to kiss them both good-bye. He remembered that Joanna was awake and giggling, and that he had played with her for a few minutes before leaving. She had seemed perfectly healthy at the time.

"About what time was that? What time was it when you last saw Joanna alive?" inquired Bonham.

Garza said it must have been about half past six in the morning, because he had to be at work at seven.

"Was anyone else in the house besides Diana and the other baby when you left?"

Garza said that no one else was there. He had gone to work as usual and was on the job when he received a message to go to the personnel office.

"And what time did you receive that message, do you remember?"

He remembered well. It was around ten o'clock that morning. He said he immediately walked over to the personnel office and found Diana waiting there. She told him that Joanna had had a "seizure" and that she had rushed her to the hospital but that she had just died. Diana was very upset. She was crying, and she even fainted in his arms. In spite of his own grief, he had done his best to comfort her.

The investigators had brought copies of the children's medical records with them, and Bailey looked at Joanna's death certificate to check the time of death.

"This says she died at the Parmer County Community Hospital at seven o'clock that morning, only a half-hour after you left for work."

Garza didn't understand; he slowly shook his head as if to clear his confusion. He said that when he saw Diana at ten o'clock, she told him that the baby had just died.

"Do you know if Joanna ever had any seizures before the day she died?"

Diana had rushed the baby to the hospital a few days earlier while he was at work, because she had had a seizure and had stopped breathing. Diana told him that the doctor thought that the child might have epilepsy.

"Well, did anyone else besides Diana ever see Joanna have a seizure?"

Garza said he didn't think so.

The deputy pulled out a copy of the hospital record of that earlier episode. It was dated November 27, 1976, and read: "This three-month-old Latin American female was discovered by her mother to be not breathing. [The mother said that] the child had been ill recently with an upper respiratory infection of one kind or another and had been seen by Dr. Pace in Farwell and had been taking some medication prescribed by him, which was not brought along."

The report continued, "[According to the mother] . . . the child had an episode of apnea [not breathing] approximately one month previously, at which time the mother stated that the child did not breathe for an hour, but after her efforts to keep her breathing she had taken it to the emergency room in Clovis [New Mexico]. . . . At the emergency room there she was told the child was dead, but she disagreed with them and then after they worked with it, it was revived."

The deputies had already contacted the hospital in Clovis, New Mexico, to obtain a copy of the report from that episode. The clerk had checked the records all the way back to 1970, but no child by the name of Joanna Garza or Joanna Lumbrera had ever been seen at that hospital.

During the hospital visit on November 27, however, the doctor had performed a complete physical examination on baby Joanna. His report contained the results of extensive, and often painful, tests that had been run on her, and all of them showed that she was normal in every way. She had been kept overnight in the hospital for observation, then additional tests had been done the following day. They also came back with normal results. The doctor was unable to find anything wrong with the child or to explain what had caused her to stop breathing on the two occasions described by her mother.

It occurred to the deputies that the November 27 incident might have been Diana's first attempt to murder the baby—an attempt which failed.

"Was anyone with Diana when the baby stopped breathing on November 27?"

Garza said he didn't think so. Diana had told him that after she discovered that the baby wasn't breathing, she called her mother, and her mother rushed them to the hospital.

The lawmen knew that when the child died three days later, the attending doctor hadn't been able to explain what had caused her death. The only clues he had noticed were her cyanosis (blue color from lack of oxygen), a small amount of blood running out of one nostril, and a trace of vomit in her mouth.

Afterward, he had talked to Diana, and she told him that the child had a history of convulsions and that she had experienced a convulsion just before her death.

The doctor guessed that the convulsion must have caused the child to vomit and that she had been drowned in that vomit. He had listed "Strangulation Due to Aspiration of Stomach Contents" as the official cause of death on her death certificate and signed it himself. The doctor didn't know that the aspiration was not a cause of death but a result of it.

No autopsy had been ordered on the child, because no one had been suspicious. That was the way it worked in Texas.

In most places in Texas, when a child dies at home, its body must not be moved until the local justice of the peace (J.P.) goes to the home and conducts an informal inquest. The inquest consists of inspecting the body for any signs of violence and talking to any witnesses. If the J.P. finds anything suspicious about the death, he can order an autopsy. If the death seems to be from natural causes, he can make that ruling and sign the death certificate. No further investigation will be conducted.

If a child who has just died is brought to a doctor, and the doctor is suspicious about the cause of the child's death, he can call the J.P. to come and conduct an inquest. After the inquest, the J.P. will once again decide whether or not to order an autopsy.

However, if the doctor thinks the child died from natural causes, then he can list what he thinks caused the death on the death certificate and sign it. No further questions will be asked.

There are two huge flaws in this system. First, justices of the peace are ordinary people who have been elected to office. They are not doctors, nor do they have any training in forensic medicine. If there are no obvious signs of violence and the witnesses sound believable, the deaths are generally signed off as natural and nothing further is done.

The second flaw is that there is no coordination

of information between counties, or even from one J.P. to the next. Many times old records are simply stored in somebody's garage, waiting to be thrown away after the retired J.P. dies. A mother could murder fifty babies if she moved around a lot, didn't leave marks on their bodies, and told a convincing story.

As the investigators listened to Tony Garza, they were looking for answers to three questions.

First, had Diana been alone with each baby when it stopped breathing? In baby Joanna's case the answer appeared to be yes. Second, had the doctors been able to explain what had caused the child to stop breathing? The answer in this case was no. Third, did Diana have a reason to want the baby dead? The answer here was maybe.

She had threatened several times to kill Joanna to get even with her young common-law husband. Could revenge have been her motive?

Bonham spoke next. "How did Diana react to Joanna's death?"

"Well, she was upset, of course," Tony replied, "and at the funeral she even fainted a couple of times. But after that she seemed okay. I remember that she even went out and bought a lot of new clothes to make herself feel better."

Bonham kept his cynicism to himself and said nothing, so Garza continued telling his story. He said that several months after Joanna died, Diana's divorce from her first husband became final, then he and Diana got married. He admitted that it was more his idea than hers; being legally married held little importance for her. Two weeks later Melissa had a near-death episode.

He and Diana had taken their two-year-old daughter to a drive-in restaurant near their home. He had stopped at the drive-through window and was talking to the cashier when Diana suddenly screamed that Melissa was having a seizure. As he spun around in the seat, he heard the child gasp for breath. Then he saw that her body was limp and her lips were blue. Terrified, he jammed the car into gear and raced toward the closest hospital, which was the Parmer County Community Hospital in nearby Friona.

As he drove, he noticed that Diana was holding the child's body tightly with one arm and pressing her face against her breast with the other. He yelled at her to be careful and to give the child some air. He drove the old car so fast and hard that its engine burned up, and it stopped running two blocks from the hospital. He swung it into the curb, grabbed Melissa, and raced the rest of the way on foot. She was teetering on the edge of death as he ran in the emergency room door.

Garza's voice was trembling, so he paused and took a deep breath. Showing emotion seemed to embarrass him, so he looked away, cleared his throat and sat up straight. The lawmen acted like they hadn't noticed.

Garza said he and Diana waited alone in a nearby room while the doctors worked on the child. Then one of them finally came out and told them that Melissa was okay. Diana wanted to take the child home, but the doctor insisted on keeping her at the hospital overnight so that tests could be run. He said that without the tests there was no way to determine what had caused her to stop breathing.

The lawmen hadn't known about this incident, because the hospital hadn't given them a copy of the medical records that had been made at the time.

"Did they find out what was wrong with her?" Bailey asked.

"No. The tests showed that she was perfectly healthy."

Exactly nine months later Diana gave birth to their son, José Luís. And once again her family celebrated the birth of another grandchild—this one being special because he was a boy. Garza knew that another newborn meant more work, less money, and less fun for Diana, but she had wanted to become pregnant with the child. He thought that proved that she wanted the baby. Otherwise, why would she have become pregnant? Anyway, she hadn't seemed resentful of José Luís like she had of Joanna.

The lawmen wondered why Diana had wanted to get pregnant with this child, since it was likely that she had already murdered Joanna and tried to murder Melissa.

Garza said that when José Luís was only two and a half months old, he received a message at work one day telling him that his son had stopped breathing and that his wife had taken him to the hospital in Muleshoe. The message said for him to meet her at Methodist Hospital in Lubbock, where the child was being transferred by ambulance for additional treatment. Garza was frantic and rushed to Lubbock to be with Diana and the baby.

He remembered that during the first two days of José's stay in the hospital, he had stayed with Diana by the baby's bedside. Then on the morning of the third day, the doctor assured him that the baby was doing fine, so he decided to return to work. He desperately needed to earn some money.

He worked the day shift as usual, then drove to his mother-in-law's house in Bovina a little after three o'clock that afternoon. At four he received a telephone call from Diana. She said that José had suffered another convulsion and was probably going to die.

Garza was shocked, because the child had been so healthy that same morning, but he quickly showered and frantically drove for two hours to Lubbock to be with them. He arrived at the hospital shortly after seven o'clock, and Diana met him at the door. She told him that José was dead. Garza was devastated.

He and Diana took the elevator up to the intensive care unit (ICU) on the second floor, where their son had died. He was surprised to find that the doctors and nurses were still there in the baby's room. They made him and Diana wait in a nearby room for a few minutes, then they were allowed to go in and see their son one last time.

Yeager pulled out the child's medical records and quickly scanned them. The report from Methodist Hospital in Lubbock contained information that the child had been brought into the hospital in

Muleshoe early Friday morning in a cyanotic condition. The doctors there had barely managed to resuscitate the baby, and even though they had examined him thoroughly, they weren't able to determine what had caused him to stop breathing.

They had transferred him by ambulance to Methodist Hospital, where he could receive specialized care under the direction of Dr. George Rich, a highly skilled and respected area pediatrician. Dr. Rich performed extensive tests on the child, but he wasn't able to explain José's condition either. He ordered that the child be moved to the ICU for close observation until a better diagnosis could be made.

The child was moved into the ICU as ordered, then electrodes were placed on his chest so that his heart rate could be monitored at all times. The monitoring was done by a technician who sat at a station in the middle of the ICU.

Yeager found a chart in the baby's file that showed the baby's heart rate at four-hour intervals during the entire time that he was attached to those electrodes. As he studied it, he made a startling discovery. During the early-morning hours of the baby's second day in the ICU, José's heart rate had suddenly increased erratically and had then slowly returned to normal.

Why? Had Diana been in the room alone with the baby when that happened? Had she tried to suffocate him again, not realizing that the electrodes would signal an alarm when the baby's heart rate began to race?

The monitoring tech had immediately notified the nurse, and the nurse raced to the baby's cubicle. The investigators would later learn that when the nurse entered the room, she found Diana leaning over the crib. Diana quickly stepped back, and the baby started crying.

The records showed that the nurse had examined the child, but except for its labored breathing, all she had found was a small trickle of blood coming from one of its nostrils. She noted the incident in the child's chart, but it obviously hadn't created any suspicions about the mother's behavior in her mind. The incident was soon forgotten, since there was no further mention of it in the reports.

"Do you remember if you left the baby's room during the early-morning hours on the second day he was there?" asked the ranger.

Garza couldn't remember. He said he might have left for a few minutes to use the rest room or something.

Yeager continued reading the report. By two o'clock on the afternoon of the third day, the child had appeared to be so healthy that Dr. Rich had ordered him transferred to the pediatrics unit. But the medical record showed that the child had died five hours later, while still in the ICU. The time given on the death certificate was 7:10 P.M. What had happened to the child during that five-hour period? And if he had died while still in the ICU as the report said, then why hadn't the electrodes, which were monitoring his heart rate, sent out another distress signal to the monitoring tech on duty?

"The baby's death certificate shows that he didn't die until a little after seven o'clock that evening, three hours after Diana telephoned you in Bovina. You didn't know that?"

Garza's eyes widened as he shook his head. He was shocked to learn that his son had still been alive when he arrived at the hospital that night, and he had a hard time controlling the emotions triggered by that information.

The lawmen exchanged knowing glances. Diana must have intended to kill the boy as soon as he was transferred out of the ICU, which she thought would occur early that afternoon. She had no idea that it would be nearly five hours before the transfer took place.

Yeager searched the file to find the report that had been made by the doctors following the Code Blue that night. What he found was dark and smudged, but he could see that the child's condition had been normal until 6:50 P.M. It was at that time that the Code Blue started.

He called a break in the interview, and while Garza visited with his family in the reception area, the three investigators stretched their legs and discussed the significance of the man's statements.

Garza's statement about receiving Diana's "death alert" call at four o'clock provided a crucial piece of evidence when added to the child's medical records, which showed that the child had been healthy until nearly three hours later. The three men could feel their excitement building.

However, experience had taught them that old

memories, along with medical records from years past, probably wouldn't be enough to get a conviction. They knew that a smart defense lawyer could convince a jury that memories faded with time and that errors in medical records were sometimes made by busy nurses who failed to notice a change in a patient's condition. That alone would be enough to establish "reasonable doubt" in the minds of jurors.

The attorney prosecuting this case would need the testimony of a nurse who had been on duty that afternoon and who could remember exactly what had happened. It would have to be someone who could testify from firsthand knowledge that the child had been healthy at four o'clock and that Diana had had the opportunity to kill it shortly before it was found cyanotic.

If they could find such a witness, they would have a real break in this particular case. And a break in one case would help in proving the others. Still, they knew that the odds against finding a person who could remember the details of an event that had taken place twelve years earlier were enormous.

One of the men retrieved Garza from the reception area while another got a cup of coffee for him. Soon they were all seated and ready to resume the interview. Garza didn't know what the lawmen were thinking, but he was having his own thoughts about what might have caused the deaths of his children. And he found those thoughts terrifying. He slowly continued telling his story.

He said Diana had told him that José died from pneumonia, which surprised him, because earlier she had told him that she had taken José to the Muleshoe hospital because he was having convulsions. He questioned Diana about the pneumonia, and she said that José must have caught it when he was transferred from Muleshoe to Lubbock.

The child's medical records showed that the doctor at the hospital in Muleshoe had run a series of tests on the infant but hadn't been able to determine why the child had stopped breathing.

The doctor had written in his report: "two month old male child in acute distress. Mother stated the child started having convulsions 24 hours prior. The convulsion consists of jerking of right upper and lower extremities. Child became cyanotic. Mother did state that she had another child that died at approximately two months of age with same problem. On admission patient was bleeding slightly from both nostrils and had increased respiratory rate [its breathing was labored]. Appeared very irritable. Mother very apprehensive."

At the bottom of the report was his final diagnosis. It read: "Convulsive disorder etiology unknown," which meant he had no idea what had caused the convulsions the child's mother had described to him.

The medial records from the hospital in Lubbock showed that the day after the child died, an autopsy had been performed on his body by the hospital pathologist, Dr. Hal Charnofsky. He had been unable to determine the cause of the child's death. The original autopsy report was missing, but a summary of that autopsy was still in the child's file, and under the heading "Cause of Death" was written the word "Undetermined."

Dr. Charnofsky had no background in forensic medicine, which meant that he had not been trained to recognize the signs of suffocation by smothering.

The hospital tests that had been performed on the child while he was still alive showed that he had a tiny amount of pneumonia in his right lung. It was the only thing Dr. Rich had found wrong with the child, but he knew that it wasn't severe enough to have caused the child's death. However, when he signed the death certificate, he wrote that the cause of death was "Sudden Infant Death Syndrome due to Pneumonia."

Sudden infant death syndrome, sometimes called "crib death," occurs when a baby, who is somewhere between two and four months of age and who is not being touched, stops breathing for some reason that doctors are unable to explain. The heart keeps pumping until the oxygen is gone from the bloodstream, then the heart stops and the child dies.

Pneumonia is a disease process caused by an infection in the lungs, and most experts believe that if the infant has pneumonia, it does not die of sudden infant death syndrome. And if it dies of sudden infant death syndrome, it should not have pneumonia.

There is one other important characteristic of SIDS. SIDS babies don't turn blue, yet this infant was very blue when the nurse ran in and discovered him not breathing.

Many doctors use SIDS as their diagnosis when

the exact cause of an infant's death isn't understood, because it's an easy answer. It relieves them of the responsibility of having to look further; it allows them to avoid facing the uncomfortable possibility that a parent might have intentionally killed his or her child.

"Was Diana at home alone that Friday morning when José stopped breathing? I mean before she first took him to the hospital in Muleshoe?" asked one of the deputies.

Garza felt sure that she had been alone because of the story she had told him afterward.

Two of the investigators' questions had already been answered: first, Diana had been alone with the boy, and second, the doctors had not been able to determine what had caused him to stop breathing. Only one question remained.

"Did Diana have any reason to want that baby dead?"

If it was a brutal question, Tony Garza didn't notice. He took the question seriously and searched his mind for an answer. And while the lawmen waited for his reply, they wondered if José's resuscitation at the hospital in Muleshoe had foiled a second attempt by Diana to murder one of her children. And they wondered if she had tried and failed yet again during the early-morning hours of the boy's second day at Methodist Hospital in Lubbock.

Finally, Garza broke the silence. He said he didn't know of any reason why Diana would have wanted his son dead. He didn't think that she had been particularly angry at him just before José's death, so if she had killed the child it wouldn't have been for revenge.

And he too wanted to know why she would have killed his son, so he looked at the three lawmen for an answer, but they had nothing to offer. They were as much in the dark as he was.

More seconds passed, then Garza looked down at the floor and continued. He said he and Diana separated a few months later, and six months after that he learned of Melissa's death. He was recovering from back surgery in an Amarillo hospital when his mother came in one afternoon and told him that Melissa had died. He said he did not know anything about her death, not for sure.

However, the investigators did. They knew that at about nine o'clock on the morning of October 2, 1978, Diana had driven to the home of a young neighbor in Bovina. She parked in front of the house, then got out of the car holding Melissa tightly in her arms. The child was cyanotic.

Diana knocked on the front door, then told the woman that Melissa was sick and asked her if she and her mother would drive them to the Parmer County Community Hospital. She said the brakes on her own car were bad, and she was afraid to make the drive herself. The woman's mother lived a short distance away, so the two women quickly walked to her house.

Once they arrived, the mother willingly helped them; in less than a minute they were on their way to the hospital. The mother had her daughter drive while she held Melissa in her own arms; she could see that Melissa wasn't breathing. Suddenly the child's body became rigid, then went limp again as a trickle of vomit spilled from the corner of her mouth. The woman knew it was the death seizure and that Melissa had just died.

Once they reached the hospital, Diana grabbed the dead child and raced into the hospital emergency room screaming for someone to save her baby. The horrified older woman and her daughter followed Diana inside, then waited with her while the doctors worked to revive the child. The two women couldn't understand why Melissa had died, because they had seen her playing outside the previous afternoon and she had looked so healthy.

The doctors tried their best to save Melissa, but their efforts were in vain; she had been dead too long to resuscitate.

The three lawmen guessed that Diana had already learned her lesson. If she wanted her victims to stay dead, she had to kill them, then wait for a while before taking them to the hospital. That was why she had driven to her neighbors for help instead of calling for an ambulance. She needed to create a reasonable delay.

The doctors did not find anything visible that would explain why Melissa had stopped breathing, and some of the medical staff, including Dr. Bruce Purdy and Dr. Allen Pace, were already suspicious of the deaths of Diana's children. They asked that the justice of the peace be contacted and an autopsy ordered.

The pathologist who performed that autopsy was Dr. Alvino Gonzalez, but, like the pathologist for José Luís, Gonzalez had no training in forensic medicine. All he could find was a bit of congestion in Melissa's lungs and a trace of vomit in her mouth and throat. He listed the cause of her death as "Asphyxia due to Aspiration of Stomach Contents." He declared her death to be from natural causes.

Once again Diana had been alone with a child when she stopped breathing, so the same question remained: "Why?" What could possibly have been Diana's motive for killing this child?

"Can you think of any reason why Diana would have wanted to kill Melissa?"

But again Garza said no. It was beyond his ability to understand this woman who had given birth to four of his children.

Inside Melissa's file, which the investigator was holding, were copies of her funeral documents. One of them had already caught his interest; it was a note from the funeral home regarding a life insurance policy on Melissa that had existed at the time of her death.

These three lawmen knew that the Garden City investigators thought Diana had murdered her last son for the life insurance money which would be left after his funeral expenses had been paid. Could "monetary gain" have also been the motive for some of the Texas murders? That possibility had seemed too farfetched to them before, not only because it would be such an incredibly unnatural act but also because so little money had probably been left over after each death. They wondered if a mother, *any* mother, could actually murder her child just to get her hands on such a small sum?

However, with no other motives turning up for José's and Melissa's deaths, the Texas lawmen decided that it was time to take a closer look into Diana's financial affairs.

"Did you have any life insurance on your children?"

Garza said that each of his children had had small life insurance policies, which he had obtained through his place of employment.

"And Diana knew that the policies existed?"

"Yes."

"Was there ever any money left over from the insurance monies after the burial expenses were paid?"

He said that when Joanna died there had been some money left. And their church had taken up a collection for them, which had totaled more than $1,000. So, yes, there had been quite a bit of money left over.

He remembered that there had also been some money left over after José's burial, but not as much because the church had not helped again. He didn't know about the money for Melissa and Melinda. He and Diana had been separated when they had died.

"Do you know if Diana had a lot of debts around the time Melissa died?" one of the other men asked.

Garza didn't know, but he said Diana had always

liked to spend money and that it was easy for her to pile up a lot of bills.

Garza was a simple man, but he wasn't stupid. He understood the connection between their questions about leftover insurance money and Diana's debts. He didn't voice his thoughts, but they were apparent to the three men who were watching him.

There was another document in Melissa's file, which the investigator didn't need to discuss with Garza. It was for Melissa's headstone, which Diana had refused to purchase. Garza had paid for it himself. The simple inscription read:

> Melissa L. Garza
> March 14, 1975
> October 2, 1978
> "Darling we miss Thee"

But Garza's story wasn't quite finished. He said that some time after Melissa died Diana came to see him. She was broke and out of work, and she begged him to help her. With some trepidation, he let her move in with him, and within a month she became pregnant with their fourth child, Melinda. Not surprisingly, it was then that their life together became a living hell.

The lawmen would learn from other sources exactly how bad things got between Tony and Diana during that period. Even though she was pregnant, she started going out with her girlfriends again, sometimes not coming home until the early morning hours. Parmer County was "dry," which meant no alcohol could be sold there, so they would go to bars in nearby "wet" counties like Castro and Hereford.

Diana quickly gained the reputation of being the pretty woman who was wild, sexual, unpredictable, and sometimes even violent. She was also a person one wouldn't want to cross.

Tony wasn't aware of Diana's reputation or the behavior that had created it. But he still strongly objected to her going out at night with her friends.

Garza admitted that he had felt powerless and shamed by her behavior. He said he begged her to go see a priest with him. She initially refused, but he continued to plead, and she eventually agreed. Their session with the priest didn't help. Diana became so enraged at the priest that she told him that their problems were none of his business. Then she jumped up and screamed at Garza that he wasn't even the father of the unborn baby she was carrying. It had been a nightmare for Garza, and he had finally had enough. He packed up and left, then obtained a legal divorce shortly afterward. That was the end of his involvement with Diana Lumbrera.

Garza said he had heard that she had given birth to the child and named her Melinda. Then, less than three years after that, he was contacted by a family member and told that the child had suddenly died. He had remarried and was living in East Texas at the time, but he returned to Bovina to attend the funeral. He said he never knew the circumstances surrounding the child's death.

The investigators thought they had obtained all the information they could from this man, so they had his statement typed up for his signature while he waited.

Minutes later the statement was ready, and Garza signed it, then stood up and prepared to leave. But before he left he shook hands with the three lawmen and shared with them a terrible burden of guilt he had kept hidden for the past twelve years.

He said that after José Luís's death, Diana had convinced him that something was genetically wrong with him and that he had passed the defect on to their children. It was that defect which had caused their deaths. When he remarried, he was terrified that someday his children from that marriage would also die. He had carried that fear with him every day of his life since the oldest of the four children was born.

Garza's face showed a mixture of relief and outrage as he said good-bye and walked out of the room. As they watched him leave, there was no doubt left in any of their minds that Diana had murdered the children.

Chapter 12

The three lawmen decided on their next course of action. Yeager would search for a witness from Methodist Hospital in Lubbock. Bailey and Bonham would continue to dig for information on the last three children who had died in Texas while in Diana's care and on any life insurance policies that had existed on any of the children.

Yeager had other cases requiring his attention, so it was Tuesday, May 29, before he began to look for a witness from Methodist Hospital. But when he did, he hit pay dirt. He located the nurse who had been on duty in the intensive care unit at the time of José Luís's death. His name was Manuel Rodriquez, and he was still employed at the same hospital. Yeager arranged to meet him at the Lubbock office of the Texas Rangers two days later.

Into Yeager's small office had been crowded a large wooden desk, a credenza, three chairs, one filing cabinet, and a computer stand. Deer horns, on which was hung Yeager's white Stetson, were mounted on the back of the door. The ranger was talking on the telephone when Rodriquez arrived, so he motioned for him to sit in one of the chairs.

Rodriquez was a solidly built man with pleasant features and a soft voice. He seemed eager to help but very surprised that the child's death was the focus of a murder investigation.

Hanging up, the ranger said in his Texas drawl, "Manuel, tell me what you remember about the day the Garza baby died. That was on February 13, 1978." The ranger prayed that the man had a good memory.

Rodriquez nodded his head, took a breath, then sighed before he spoke. It was obvious that this was a memory which brought back uncomfortable feelings.

"I remember the child's death very well," he said sadly. "I teach in the nurses' training program at the hospital, and I've used it for years as an example of how a patient can seem normal one minute and go critical the next. You know, I've never understood why that child died, and it's always haunted me.

"Anyway, I was about twenty-six-years-old at the time, and I'd been working at the hospital for three years. My assignment was the Medical Intensive Care Unit ward, and my shift began at three o'clock in the afternoon.

"The baby had come to us with seizures that Friday and had been admitted by Dr. Rich, our head pediatrician. The baby had done fine all weekend long. On Monday, when I came on duty, he was still in the

ICU, but Dr. Rich had already left orders that he was to be moved to the pediatrics ward as soon as a bed was available. It generally takes a while before a room is assigned to someone moving out of the ICU, because it's such a big hospital.

"The rooms in the ICU are really glass-enclosed cubicles, with curtains that can be pulled when a patient is being attended and privacy is needed. The rooms line the walls of the ICU, and two stations, actually desk areas, sit in the center: a nurses' station, where I sit when I work, and a monitoring station about ten feet away that is manned by a monitoring tech.

"Well, as soon as I got to work that day I made a physical assessment of all the patients in the unit and recorded their conditions in my nurse's notes. I remember that when I checked the Garza baby that day all of his vital signs were good; his condition appeared to be perfectly normal. He was full of energy, and I remember that he cried when I checked on him."

"Was his mother in there with him at the time?"

"No, she didn't come in until about an hour later, a little after four o'clock. In ICU we have limitations on our visitors, but when the patient is a baby, we let parents come in and go out as they please. We always keep a chair by the crib so that they can sit there with him when they want."

"And the baby was fine when you checked him at four o'clock? You're sure of that?" Yeager asked, leaning forward.

"Oh, yes. The baby was fine. Well, when the

baby's mother came in she stopped at the nurses' station and asked me how he was doing, you know, the normal things a mother would ask: How is he doing? Is he running a temperature? That sort of thing. I told her, 'Your baby is doing quite well.' So, she went into the baby's room and sat down by him, then she stayed there. I felt very good about her being in there with him, because babies always want their mothers to be with them; it makes them feel more secure.

"I continued to check on the baby about every thirty minutes, even though there were electrodes connected to his chest that allowed a monitor tech to constantly monitor his heartbeat."

"And the baby's condition remained good during that entire time?"

"Yes, the baby continued to do very well," replied the nurse.

Yeager relaxed back into his chair, but he didn't allow his elation to show on his face. He was a man who held his feelings close to the vest.

"Then, by six o'clock," continued the nurse, completely unaware of the importance of his knowledge, "a room had been assigned to the baby, so I began to prepare the paperwork needed for the transfer. I noticed that he had started to fuss with the electrodes and was trying to pull them off, so I went in and took them off myself." The nurse coughed nervously once or twice and glanced away before continuing.

"Did his mother ask you to take them off?"

"No, I—I did it because of his discomfort, and

since I was about to move him it was not unusual to do that. So I took off the patches, which took him off the monitor, then I went back to the nurses' station. Minutes later when I looked through the window at him, I could see that he was falling asleep.

"At six-thirty I checked him again. He was asleep, his color was good, and his mother was with him, so when I left the room that time, I turned out the lights.

"There aren't any outside windows in the rooms, but even with the lights out you can still see the silhouettes inside the rooms. So, when I got back to the nurses' station I saw the mother get up and stand over the baby's crib."

"Could you make out what she was doing?"

"Well, it looked like she was loving him, you know, touching his face the way most parents do when their child is sick. She had her left arm on the bed above his head and was touching his face with her right hand."

"Now, were you watching her the whole time?"

"No, I had to go get the baby's medications, do my last-minute charting, and finish getting everything ready to move him, because by that time it was quarter to seven.

"Well, I had returned to the nurses' station and was working on the chart when all of a sudden his mother ran out of his room and then raced out of the unit."

"Did she know you were there?"

"Yes. She knew I was there, because I was right

in front of her, but she didn't say anything to me," the nurse said with growing emotion. "She was holding her hands up to her face like this, like she was crying, and she just ran to the door and left. That was the unusual thing—for her to leave rather than to ask me for help if something was wrong with the child."

The nurse paused for a moment to examine her behavior in this new light.

"Well, did her running out that way make you suspicious?" asked the ranger.

"Suspicious? No, it wasn't that it made me suspicious, because who would think that a young mother would intentionally hurt her baby?"

Yeager just nodded his head. It occurred to him that this kind of response was one reason why Diana had managed to get away with her crimes for so long.

"Look, I'm not a parent," the nurse continued, needing to be understood, "but if I had a child, and if that child was in trouble, I would go to that person who could help my child. But she didn't do that, and that's what made the whole thing so unusual."

"Okay, what did you do then?"

"I got up and rushed into the baby's room, because I could feel that something was wrong, and when I turned on the light, I saw that the baby was blue. I checked for a pulse, but there was no pulse or respiration, so I called out for help and started CPR and mouth-to-mouth. Another nurse on the unit heard me and put out a Code Blue, then others ran in to help.

"I know a nurse is supposed to always keep it together, but I just couldn't understand, and I lost my composure. I kept saying, 'This can't be. The baby was fine!' hoping that someone or something could explain why this had happened. Of course, no one could.

"Dr. Rich was paged, but before he got there, one of the other doctors ran in to help. He put a tube into the baby's lungs so that we could manually breathe him while someone else hooked him up to the monitor. He had no heart rhythm. Of course, I continued the chest compressions. The baby was given the standard injections."

"What kind of injections?" Yeager had already read the statements that Diana had made to the Kansas investigators, and he remembered that she had said that this baby had died because of an injection it had just received. He didn't want to leave any loose ends in this case.

"He was given Adrenalin to stimulate the heart and sodium bicarb to bring the pH back into the normal range so that the heart would be more susceptible to treatment."

"Okay, go on," directed the ranger after jotting on the writing pad in front of him.

"Well, Dr. Rich arrived within five to ten minutes after we started, then we all worked for another twenty minutes or so before we finally accepted the fact that the baby was gone. Dr. Rich was in charge, so he was the one who called off the Code Blue."

The ranger asked the nurse how much time he thought had elapsed between the time the baby's breathing had stopped and when he had discovered that the baby was blue.

"Well, by the time the mother ran out, it was just a matter of seconds until I ran in there. You know, death is a gradual process, and it takes some time. You don't lose your color immediately; it takes about five minutes before the body turns blue. And you still have some movement for a while. Then at the end there is always one last seizure. It might be a violent seizure, or it may be a very mild one, but it always happens.

"So with the baby's mother being at the bedside with him, cuddling him as I thought she was doing, she would have known that something was wrong with the baby prior to his death. That's why I kept wondering why she hadn't called me. You know, she told us that the baby had seizured when she was with him, so why didn't she call me to help?"

"What happened then?"

"Afterward, Dr. Rich questioned me about what had happened, and I told him. But, once again, I couldn't explain *why* it had happened, because the baby had been perfectly normal just a short time before. I was just in a state of awe by that time, because nothing made any sense. It was all so bizarre."

"Did Dr. Rich have any suspicion that the baby's mother might have caused its death?"

"No, he was just as confused as I was. None of us ever suspected that foul play might have been involved."

"Did she try to come back into the room when the Code Blue was going on?"

"That I don't know. However, we never let family members remain when we're still working on a patient. We generally send a nurse to stay with the family until it's over and we're ready to allow them back into the room."

"Do you know where she went to wait?"

"She and her husband were in the waiting room, which is right outside the unit, if I remember correctly."

"Who went to get her after it was over?"

"Dr. Rich and I both went to speak to them. Dr. Rich told them that he had been unable to save the baby, and of course, she was crying and acting like a normal mother would—you know, very emotionally. I felt so badly for her. I remember that I embraced her and told her how sorry I was."

"What happened after that? Did the husband ask any questions?"

"No. Dr. Rich asked them for their permission to do an autopsy, and they gave it. Then once the baby's body was ready, we let them go back and view it. We also got the information we needed, such as which funeral home they wanted to use, then the nursing supervisor called the funeral home for them."

"Did they want to see the baby?"

"Yes. They both wanted to see him, and she was very emotional in the room with his body. Then, after they left, the nursing supervisor took the body down to the morgue, which is in the basement of the hospital. That was the last of my involvement with the child and his family. I never saw them again."

"And the autopsy . . . ?"

"Well, it was performed the day after the baby died. It was done by the hospital pathologist in the autopsy room of the morgue. I didn't see the autopsy report, but I remember reading Dr. Rich's notes, which said that only a nosebleed and a small amount of pneumonia in the child's lungs had been found."

"Do you remember what was listed as the official cause of death?"

"I was told that the autopsy results ended in 'Undetermined,' and since nothing could be found to explain the child's death, Dr. Rich listed 'Sudden Infant Death Syndrome' on its death certificate."

While the nurse looked on in silence, Yeager finished writing up his notes. When he was done, the nurse continued talking.

"You know," he said, looking downward, "I've always felt a lot of guilt about that child's death, because if I had only left him on the monitor until I moved him, we could have caught it. That's always been on my mind, the what-if. It's always stayed in my mind that something was not right about how the baby died."

The interview was over, so Yeager had a secretary type up the nurse's statement. Then, after the man had signed it, Yeager took the time to reassure him that the child's death had not been his fault. He told him about the phone call that Diana had made to her husband at four o'clock on the afternoon of the child's death, the one in which she had said that the baby was dying three hours before it actually did.

After the nurse left, Yeager made a quick call to the deputies to tell them he had found a witness, a very good witness, who had been able to answer all their questions and who would do very well on the witness stand. Yeager also explained why the electrodes hadn't sent out an alarm when the child was dying; the nurse had taken them off as an act of kindness toward the infant and his mother.

It was a good moment for the lawmen; they felt as though things were finally beginning to fall into place. One of them speculated on the relief Diana must have felt when the kind nurse took the electrodes off the baby's chest and turned off the lights, giving her the chance she needed to kill José. It occurred to him how strange it was that she never thought anyone would suspect her in the child's death. The sad irony was that she was right.

Chapter 13

While Yeager was interviewing Nurse Rodriquez, Bailey and Bonham were collecting information on Diana's fourth victim, Ericka Aleman, the six-week-old daughter of her cousins, Ben and Karen.

Bailey found Karen Aleman living in a small duplex apartment on a dirt street in a little town south of Lubbock. She was a large woman in her early forties, with thick, graying hair worn in a long braid that reached past her waist. She looked tired and worn, but she was willing to talk. She invited the deputy inside and fixed him a cup of coffee.

She told the deputy about her days with Ben Aleman and about their decision to have one last child. She spoke about Diana and her eight-month-old daughter moving in with them before the baby was born. She remembered that October day when Diana had picked up little Ericka and said she was going to take her to a doctor in Muleshoe. That confused Karen, because the baby was in perfect health.

Karen leaned forward and placed her elbows on the worn oilcloth that covered the table; a heaviness seemed to settle on her shoulders. She said that about an hour and a half later, relatives of Ben's came to her home and told her that her baby had died. They rushed her and Ben to the hospital, but they had to wait before they could see their child. She became angry and demanded to know where Diana was, but no one knew. She went looking for Diana and finally found her in the rest room.

"I was angry, and I said to her, 'What happened?' and she told me she was sorry, but it happened so fast. She said the baby let out a scream and stopped breathing when she was about twenty minutes from the house and that the closest hospital was twenty minutes away in Muleshoe. She said she tried her best, but it was really the doctor's fault that Ericka had died. Then when my husband and I left the hospital to go home, he asked me what I thought, and I told him I didn't know. He told me he thought the bitch had killed her."

Karen told the deputy how angry Ben had become that night, and how he beat on the refrigerator door and screamed that he knew Diana had murdered their baby. Karen said that she wasn't sure of anything that day; too much had happened, and she was too sick and hadn't been able to think clearly.

"But I knew deep down that Diana did it," Karen said angrily. "I just didn't want to face it at the time. Then later I heard that she was going 'round to everyone in the family, telling them that Ericka's death wasn't her fault. She was always such a damn liar!"

At that moment Karen's twenty-year-old daughter, Casey, popped her head through the doorway. She was a tall, slender girl, and Bailey asked her what she remembered of that day.

Casey had been ten years old when her baby sister died, and though she had vivid "feeling" memories of that day, the actual events had become a blur in her mind. Her only recollection was that after Diana had returned from the hospital, she had taken her in the car and driven off somewhere. She couldn't remember what Diana had said or done or even where they had gone during that ride. She only remembered that she had felt a lot of anxiety.

She told Bailey that she wanted to help, but she just couldn't remember anything else.

Bailey wondered why Diana had taken the ten-year-old for a ride at that particular time. Had she planned on killing this child too? Had she tried to kill her or had something changed her mind? He knew that the events of that ride might be very important to the investigation, so he made a mental note to see if there was a way to help Casey remember.

The interview ended shortly, so Bailey thanked the woman and her daughter and got up to leave. Karen was grateful that they were finally investigating the death of her child. "If I can help put that bitch away—just anything I can do to help."

Bailey gave her a reassuring smile and said,

"You bet!" Then he turned and walked back to his car. He could understand why this woman wanted Diana to pay for the lives she had ruined, because he was feeling exactly the same way. And he was outraged that no one in authority had ever stopped her.

Chapter 14

The following morning Bonham located the nurse who had been on duty at the time Diana had brought little Ericka Aleman's dead body into the hospital in Muleshoe. Her name was Julie Mullins, and she was employed by a different hospital in an adjoining county. She met the two deputies at Bailey's office in Dimmitt that same afternoon.

Nurse Mullins was a small, fragile-looking woman in her mid-fifties with long gray hair worn up in a bun. She said she had been walking down the corridor toward the reception area that October morning of 1980 when she saw the woman (Diana) walk into the building with the baby hanging limply in her arms.

The deputies wanted to make sure they had heard correctly. "You actually saw her *walk*, not run, into the hospital with the child?" one of them asked.

She said the woman had been walking; she was sure of that. The woman had been quiet until she saw the nurse looking at her, then she began screaming, "My baby is dying! Please save my baby!" The woman then rushed over to the nurse and handed her the infant.

The nurse said she saw that the baby was cyanotic, so she turned and ran toward the emergency room, where a Code Blue could be started. At that moment she saw Dr. Allen Pace walking down the corridor toward her, so she called out to him, then she and the doctor rushed into the E.R. and began working on the child.

Dr. Pace quickly examined the baby and found that she had no heartbeat, no respiration (was not breathing), and her pupils were dilated. She was completely unresponsive. He looked up at the nurse and said flatly, "This baby is dead."

The doctor asked the nurse what had happened to the baby, and she answered that she did not know. She explained about the woman who had walked in. She thought the woman was the infant's mother and that she was probably waiting outside in the corridor.

Dr. Pace opened the door and told the woman outside to come into the room. Then he asked her what had happened to the child. The nurse had been surprised at the anger in the doctor's voice, because she had not known about Diana's history of bringing dead babies into the hospital.

"Were you able to hear what they were saying?" Bailey asked.

The nurse didn't recall all that was said, but she did remember the woman saying that she had had to stop halfway to the hospital because the baby had vomited.

The nurse said that Dr. Pace opened the door, told the woman to wait outside, and closed the door behind her. Then he and the nurse checked the baby for signs of vomit, but there were none. That was when the doctor referred to the woman as Diana Lumbrera.

The nurse said that Dr. Pace went out of the room to talk to the woman again while she stayed inside to cover the baby with a white sheet. She heard the woman become hysterical, crying and screaming that she would sue the nurse, Dr. Pace, and the hospital for not saving her baby. The nurse stayed in the treatment room with the baby until the woman left. That was all she remembered of the events of that day. For the deputies, it was enough.

The deputies already knew that Dr. Pace had requested that an autopsy be performed on the child, so the justice of the peace had been called and an autopsy scheduled for later that same day. But a mix-up had occurred, and the body had been transported to the funeral home without the accompanying paperwork. The undertakers had assumed the body was being delivered for a regular burial, so they started the embalming process. By the time the mistake was discovered, embalming fluid had already been injected into the body, and that fluid had erased some of the visible clues—like the cyanosis of the baby's skin.

But that wasn't the only problem. The documented clinical information on the child, which would have included the reports on the Code Blue and Dr. Pace's suspicions, was also missing. The pathologist was Dr. Guy Wilson, a man with no forensic training, and he was left with no help and very few clues. It was like shooting in the dark.

His autopsy showed that the child's body was perfectly normal, without disease or injury, and he wasn't able to find the cause of death. He listed "Undetermined" under the heading "Cause of Death" in his report. And, in spite of the growing suspicions that many were beginning to have about Diana Lumbrera, the police were never called and no investigation into the child's death was ever initiated.

Ericka Aleman was victim number four. Diana had been alone with the child when she stopped breathing, and the doctor and the pathologist had not been able to determine any natural cause for the baby's death. But, once again, Diana's motive remained a mystery.

The lawmen hoped that the answer might lie in the forgotten memories of Casey Aleman. Yeager suggested that they ask Sergeant Joe Sanders of the Midland office of the Texas Rangers for help, since Sanders was both an investigator and a trained hypnotist. They arranged to meet with Sanders two days later.

Chapter 15

Casey Aleman, the two deputies, and Warren Yeager sat around the long conference table and watched as Joe Sanders pulled the thick draperies across the only window in the oblong room. The draperies blocked out the glare of the harsh West Texas sun and helped Casey to relax.

Sanders was a tall, barrel-chested man in his early Forties with silver hair and glasses. There was a practiced, soothing quality to his voice. He began by explaining to Casey what he was about to do and asking her to trust him. He spent nearly two hours developing a rapport with the girl, telling her about himself, his family, his job.

When he was ready to begin the hypnosis, he told her to get comfortable in her chair, shut her eyes, and relax. His words, spoken in a steady monotone, were soft and reassuring. They slowly lulled Casey into a very deep hypnotic sleep. Then he began the slow process of taking Casey back in her mind to the day of her baby sister's death.

The session lasted more than three hours, and the ranger's efforts proved effective. Casey remembered exactly what had happened that day, though what she had to tell proved to be of little value.

She said a number of relatives had come over to their home and that they had all been very emotional. She had also been upset, and it had occurred to her that Diana might have intentionally killed her sister, but she hadn't mentioned her suspicions to anyone.

Diana must have sensed Casey's suspicions, though, because shortly after she returned, she told Casey to get in her car. She told her that she was going to take her to the doctor in Bovina to get her a shot, because the shot would make her feel better.

As they were driving to Bovina, Casey asked Diana what had happened to Ericka. She asked, "Did you kill her?"

Casey remembered that Diana had replied, "No. I was taking Ericka to Muleshoe, and on the way there she let out a big scream and stretched out. I picked her up and gave her mouth-to-mouth resuscitation while I raced on to the hospital. I did my best, but the doctors weren't able to save her."

Diana also told Casey that she knew that she and her family would blame her for Ericka's death. Casey felt guilty for thinking such awful thoughts, so she quickly reassured Diana that it hadn't been her fault.

When they reached Bovina, they didn't go to the doctor. Instead, they went somewhere else, Casey didn't recognize the place, then Diana went into the building and returned with a Coke for Casey. Shortly after that they arrived back home, and that was all she could remember.

It didn't sound as though Diana had attempted to murder the girl, although that could have been her initial intention. Perhaps she decided that it would be too difficult to kill a child that old or maybe that it would be too difficult to explain away the death of a ten-year-old child. Or maybe she sensed the child's suspicions and wanted to keep her away from the others until she could change the girl's mind. Or maybe she just wanted the girl to believe in her innocence, just as she had said.

Overall, the girl's memories had proved disappointing. The three lawmen still hadn't found an answer to the question of why Diana had murdered that baby.

But Diana's motive for killing her next victim would become all too obvious, and it would provide an insight into part of her motive for murdering at least four of her own children.

Chapter 16

After baby Ericka died, Diana and her daughter, Melinda, moved back into her mother's home in Bovina. Two of Diana's sisters were also living there at the time. Diana took small temporary jobs, and in the late fall of 1981 she went to work as a waitress in a little cafe in Bovina. She was twenty-three years old. She worked hard during the day and partied hard at night. It wasn't long before Melinda had her first near-death episode.

Medical records from the hospital in Muleshoe showed that shortly before four o'clock on the morning of February 10, 1982, an ambulance rushed Melinda to the hospital's emergency room. Diana accompanied her daughter in the ambulance and upon arriving at the hospital, she told the doctor on duty that she had just found the child unconscious and blue in color. She also said that blood had been coming from the child's nose.

The ambulance attendant told the doctor that the child had been unconscious most of the way to the hospital. The child was two years and three months old, and the doctor who worked on her was Allen Pace.

Dr. Pace wrote in the child's hospital progress notes: "The history of this family is that three or four of this lady's children have died somewhat mysteriously. I'm going to check this patient out for possible trauma."

The doctor made a thorough examination of the child, but he was not able to find any natural reasons that would explain why the child had stopped breathing. Nor could he find any evidence of child abuse. Besides a small amount of pneumonia is one of the child's lungs, the only thing he could find was a small amount of blood in her nostrils. There was nothing to substantiate what he believed had caused her nosebleed.

These findings left the doctor without any tangible proof that Diana had ever abused the child or that she had just tried to kill her. The best he could do was to admit the child into the hospital for observation and for her own protection.

Two days later, in spite of his fears, the hospital was legally required to release the child into the care of her mother. One can only guess what must have been in Dr. Pace's mind when he saw that helpless child being carried out the hospital door by Diana Lumbrera.

The deputies wondered whether this incident had been another failed attempt at murder or if Diana had simply been laying the groundwork for what would soon follow. Because six months later, in August 1982, Melinda suddenly died.

Diana had still been working at the little cafe at that time, so Bailey and Bonham went in search of the people who had owned it. Their names were Jerry and Pat Ward, and the deputies found them at their home in Bovina. It was Mrs. Ward who had run the cafe, and she said she remembered Diana Lumbrera very well.

Pat Ward was a friendly, heavyset woman in her mid-fifties who obviously liked people. She said Diana had been a nice person but that she had a wild streak in her. She brought Melinda into the cafe on several different occasions during the months that she had worked there, and Mrs. Ward became familiar with the child. She said Melinda was always neat, and she never appeared to have been abused in any way.

Mrs. Ward remembered the child's death well. She said that since Melinda had always seemed so healthy it was difficult to accept her sudden death. She didn't really know, but it was still hard for her to understand why the child had died. When she asked Diana why, she replied that there had been heart trouble on her (Diana's) father's side of the family and that it was this weakness that had triggered the child's death. Melinda died of heart failure. Diana explained that Melinda had gone into convulsions early in the evening but had later fallen into a restful sleep. She said she had thought it best to let the child rest. Then during the early-morning hours she had checked on her again. It was then that she had found the child dead.

Mrs. Ward said she felt great sympathy for Diana, because she knew how hard it was for folks when they lost a child. She had tried to help out by preparing a big meal for Diana's family to eat after the funeral was over. But remembering that day brought back some troubling memories.

She talked about how surprised she had been to find that Diana wasn't very affected by Melinda's death; Diana hadn't even seemed sad after the funeral that day. And only three or four days later, Diana had started "kicking up her heels" by going out to bars with her friends. In fact, her life quickly returned to normal. Mrs. Ward said it was as if Melinda had never existed.

The woman also remembered that a few weeks after Melinda's death, Diana had borrowed $150 from her for "something that she needed." Mrs. Ward said she heard later that Diana had gone to a midwife in Hereford, Texas, and gotten an abortion.

As the interview was ending, Mrs. Ward said one more very interesting thing. She said that it was funny that Diana had needed to borrow that money from her, because she had had so much life insurance on the dead child.

"Life insurance? What do you mean by 'so much life insurance'?" asked Bonham.

Mrs. Ward said that an insurance salesman had come into the cafe the day before Melinda died, and she remembered distinctly that Diana bought an additional life insurance policy on herself and the child from him. She even remembered the agent's name, because he was a local man.

"And about what time was that, do you remember?"

She said that it was late that afternoon, probably sometime around four or five o'clock.

The two men knew that Melinda had died at one-thirty the following morning. It looked as if the guys up in Garden City, Kansas, had been right; monetary gain certainly was one of Diana's motives, at least in the murder of this child.

Mrs. Ward had been very helpful, and the two lawmen told her so, then left. They returned to Bonham's office and began to search for the insurance salesman Mrs. Ward had mentioned.

They located him at his home in Hereford, and he said he would meet them at the sheriff's office in less than an hour. He had his own reasons for wanting to share what he knew about Diana Lumbrera.

The man's name was Donald Price, and he was a dignified and well-spoken retired gentleman in his early sixties. Like so many of the other people the deputies had interviewed, he remembered Diana Lumbrera very well. He said he had been employed by the Gevalia Life and Accident Insurance Company as an agent at the time. She was working in a little cafe in Bovina, and she had her little girl with her that day.

Price had brought his records with him to the sheriff's office, so he stopped and referred to them for a moment, then continued. He said that he had met Diana at approximately four o'clock on the afternoon of August 16, 1982.

Price had introduced himself to Diana and asked her if she was interested in obtaining a life insurance policy on herself and her child. She had shown immediate interest in the idea, and he had quickly sold her a $5,000 policy on herself with a children's rider for half that amount, $2,500.

She paid him one month's premium before he left that day, which had put the policy into effect immediately. He hadn't been particularly worried about the sale, because both Diana and the child appeared to be very healthy.

He said that at five-thirty the following morning he was awakened at his home by a telephone call from Diana Lumbrera. In a calm voice she told him that her little girl had died just a few hours earlier and that she wanted him to send her the $2,500 from the child's policy.

Donald Price had been stunned by the news. It didn't make any sense to him that the healthy child he had seen on the previous afternoon had suddenly taken ill and died fewer than twelve hours after he had written a policy on her. Or that her bereaved mother had just phoned him at home at this early hour to calmly ask for the insurance policy.

As soon as his company's district offices in Amarillo opened that morning, he contacted the claims section and asked that a copy of the standard death claim form be mailed to him. He also passed along his concerns regarding the circumstances surrounding the child's death and suggested that they conduct an investigation.

When the claim form arrived at his home, he hand-carried it to Diana Lumbrera and sat there with her while he filled it out. He remembered how unemotional she was, even though her child had died only days earlier. He said he had never met a parent who had acted that way after losing a child.

His company spent about a month "investigating" the matter, then sent him a check issued to Diana Lumbrera in the amount of $2,500 plus interest.

"Frankly, I don't understand why your company paid Diana," said Bailey. "If you told them the child's death was suspicious, and if they investigated like they said they did, they must have known that Melinda was the fifth dead kid she had brought into a hospital."

The puzzled deputy stared at the agent and waited, but in his mind he was evaluating the consequences of the company's response. If that insurance company had stirred things up rather than simply paying the claim, then maybe a full-scale police investigation would have been launched. And maybe Diana would have been prevented from murdering any more children.

The retired insurance agent nodded his head in understanding. In a depressed voice he said that he had voiced his objections when he learned that his company was going to pay Diana's claim. But his words had fallen on deaf ears.

He had been told that it was just "good business" to pay the claim and forget it. To do otherwise might affect policy sales, because the public might think that the company was harassing a grieving mother. And even if the company did refuse to pay the claim, it would cost more than $2,500 to fight it out in court.

It was that simple. The company's decision had not been based on moral principles. It had been based on the financial bottom line.

Price still had strong feelings about the entire incident, which were obvious as he continued his story. He said that after receiving the check, he delivered it in person to Diana, and once again she showed absolutely no emotion over the child's death.

She never paid any more premiums on her own policy, so it was cancelled a month or two later for nonpayment. He never saw or heard from her again, but he had never forgotten her or the mysterious death of her little girl.

The agent wasn't alone in his suspicions about this child's death. Many had felt suspicious, and among them were the medical staff members at the Parmer County Community Hospital, who had tried to resuscitate the dead child that night.

The hospital records showed that at one-thirty on the morning of August 17, 1982, Diana Lumbrera had run into the hospital's emergency room carrying Melinda's limp, cyanotic body in her arms. The child, two years and nine months old, was dead on arrival.

The doctors ran a Code Blue on the child, but she had been dead too long to be revived. After

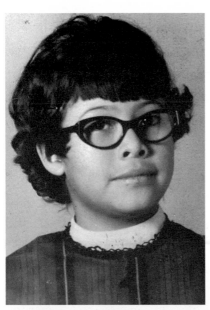

Diana Lumbrera,
age 6.

Diana, age 17,
with her first
child, Melissa.

Melissa in her coffin. She died at age 3 years, 6 months. This was the only photo Diana kept of any of her first five children.

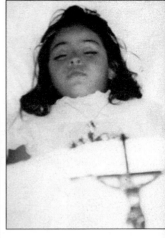

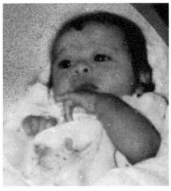

Joanna died a month after this picture was taken.

Graves of Joanna, José Luís, and Melissa. Diana spent less money on the burials as time went by.

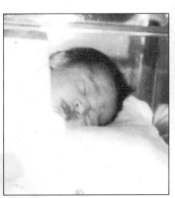

Ericka Aleman died at age 6 weeks.

Melinda Ann Garza, age 2, on her last Christmas.

Christopher, age 3 months, shortly before his death.

Diana with José Antonio, age 4. Diana smothered him a few months later. *(Photo By Maria Falcon)*

Finney County Attorney Ricklin Pierce prosecuted Diana for José Antonio's murder in Garden City, Kansas. *(Photo by James Hawkins)*

Detective Ken Elliott of Garden City Police Dept. began an investigation with Detective James Hawkins of Diana Lumbrera shortly after José Antonio's death. *(Photo by Douglas Smeltz)*

Detective James Hawkins, Garden City Police Dept. *(Photo courtesy James Hawkins)*

Undercover narcotics investigator Mike Utz of the Garden City Police Dept. assisted in the arrest of Diana Lumbrera for the murder of José Antonio. *(Photo by James Hawkins)*

Captain Charlie Armentrout,
Garden City Police Dept.
(Photo by James Hawkins)

Deputy Jerry Bailey of the
Castro County Sheriff's office
investigated the deaths of
Diana's first five children and
Ericka Aleman.

Texas Ranger Warren Yeager
was called in to investigate the
death of José Luís, Diana's second child.

Deputy Richard Bonham of
the Parmer County Sheriff's
Office began the Texas investigation.

Diana and her attorney, Mike Quint, at her first trial in Kansas. *(Photo by Dennis Lundgren, Garden City Telegram)*

Dr. William Eckert, forensic pathologist based in Wichita, Kansas, testifies for the defense. Judge Stephen Nyswonger listens in the background. *(Photo by Dennis Lundgren, Garden City Telegram)*

Diana testifies at her trial in Kansas. *(Photo by Dennis Lundgren, Garden City Telegram)*

Pediatrician Michael Shull was in charge of the Code Blue on José Antonio, Diana's last victim. His call to the police began an investigation into the deaths of all seven children.

Dr. Harry. L. Wilson, pediatric pathologist. *(Photo by Michael Ross, courtesy of Providence Memorial Hospital, El Paso, Texas)*

Dr. Eva Vachal, general pathologist. *(Photo by Ellen Thiemann, Ellen's Photography)*

Diana is booked into the Parmer County Sheriff's Office in Farwell, Texas, following her first trial in Kansas.
(Photo by Rex Williams)

Diana leaving the Parmer County courtroom after pleading nolo contendre to Melinda's murder.
(Photo courtesy <u>Castro County News</u>)

Diana being escorted to court by Lubbock sheriff's deputies. She would plead nolo contendre to the murder of José Luís.
(Photo courtesy <u>Lubbock Avalanche Journal</u>)

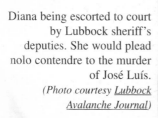

thirty minutes the code was stopped, and the child was officially declared to be dead.

The doctor's report, which was written shortly afterward, mentioned only two abnormalities on the child's body: the blue, cyanotic color of her skin and a small amount of blood coming from one of her nostrils. Nothing had been found that could explain why she had stopped breathing.

It was the death of this child that had prompted Dr. Bruce Purdy of Muleshoe to telephone the sheriff of Parmer County and demand that an investigation into the deaths of Diana Lumbrera's children be conducted.

Melinda's death also caused Dr. Purdy to contact the state Child Protective Services and discuss his suspicions at length with the person in charge. That person had told him that an investigation would be conducted, but apparently he or she had done nothing. Dr. Purdy had never heard from the agency again.

It had also been this child's death that had caused John Blackwell, the funeral director who supervised her burial, to become suspicious.

Blackwell had also called the then-elected Parmer County sheriff and voiced his concerns. But those suspicions had soon been put to rest when forensic pathologist Dr. Ralph Erdmann convinced him that the child's death was from natural causes.

Erdmann had concluded that the cause of death was "acute heart failure due to increased taxation." In his autopsy report he had written that a small amount of pneumonia in the child's lungs had created too much stress on a defective heart and that stress had caused the heart to stop. And since Erdmann's report ruled out the possibility of foul play, the authorities were never legally obligated to investigate. So they never did.

In looking over the records written at the time of the child's death, the deputies found Diana's version of what had happened that night. She said that she and the child had been sleeping alone in the living room, while her mother and two sisters were asleep in the bedrooms. She awakened when she felt the child urinate on the blankets they were sleeping on, so she turned on a light to check on her. It was then that she found her blue in color and not breathing. She said she screamed for her sisters to help her and that they ran into the living room, then helped her get the baby to the hospital. Only it was too late.

The deputies felt that this was the first Texas murder for which all three questions could clearly be answered. Diana had been alone with Melinda when she stopped breathing, the doctors had not been able to determine the real cause of death, and the motive had been to collect the life insurance. It was one of Diana's quick-money schemes.

They immediately contacted district attorney Johnny Actkinson, and when he learned what they had uncovered, he began to take seriously the possibility that Diana had murdered her children. He reorganized his work schedule to include the investigation and prosecution of possibly four serial killings. He brought in his assistant, attorney Luther

Thompson, to coordinate the efforts of his office with those of the three investigators.

In the meantime, the two deputies focused their attention on uncovering the facts surrounding the death of the sixth child who had died while in Diana's care, her five-month-old son, Christopher Daniel Lumbrera.

Chapter 17

The deputies learned that after Melinda's death in August 1982, Diana continued to live in her mother's home in Bovina, although she spent a great deal of time in the company of the various men she was dating. As a rule, Diana wouldn't date Caucasians; she apparently felt unsure of herself when she was with them. She dated only Hispanic men, and she preferred the ones who had just come up from Mexico. It seemed to others that she could more easily control them, because they didn't speak English. She could get them to spend money on her. She and some of her girlfriends would find them at the sleaziest Mexican bars, then often take them to parties at one of their homes. Fueled by booze, they would dance and party till daybreak. When the men's money ran out, the party was over.

Ben Aleman, Diana's cousin, saw one of her wild parties firsthand. One night when his mother was out of town, Diana and one of her girlfriends picked up four or five men at a local bar, stopped and bought several cases of beer, then drove to Ben's mother's house in Dimmitt. Diana had a key, so they all went inside, pulled the shades, cranked up the music, passed around the booze and started dancing. The party was just moving into high gear when Ben pulled his car into the driveway. When he saw what was happening, he was outraged. He scolded Diana harshly for using his mother's home in that way. Then he made the men leave. He stood in the doorway and watched in disgust as the men slowly straggled out to their cars.

It was during this time that Diana allegedly figured out a way to make some more quick money. According to people who knew her at the time, she began contacting men who were still in Mexico and arranging for them to come across the border illegally. She even talked at least one of her girlfriends into marrying one of them, so that he could get a work card legally. The men allegedly paid Diana very well for this service. Then afterward she would date them until she got whatever money they had left or until her violence frightened them away. It was easy work for a woman who liked to party and who apparently enjoyed hurting men.

Diana's aging mother didn't approve of her behavior, and one night she told her so. She said decent women didn't act like that and demanded that Diana stop. But Diana didn't care about other people's opinions. She grabbed her things, stuffed them into an old suitcase, and told her mother not to interfere in her life if she ever wanted to see her again. Then she slammed out the door. A week later Diana returned, put her things away, and acted as if she had never left. Her mother said nothing and never dared to criticize her daughter again.

Only five months had passed since Melinda's death when Diana became pregnant again, and she decided to have this baby. She waited until August 1983, then using the name Diana Marcos, she went to a doctor in a small new medical clinic in Muleshoe. She told the doctor she was feeling movement in her stomach and that she hadn't missed a period but was wondering if she could be pregnant. The doctor examined her and reported that he believed her to be nearly seven months pregnant.

This didn't surprise Diana. She had already been to Dr. Bruce Purdy's office, where she had had a pregnancy test that was positive. It was during that visit that Dr. Purdy had refused to be her doctor because he was convinced she was killing her children.

Diana visited the second doctor because she apparently intended to use this baby to extort money from a man she knew, and to do that she needed a doctor's report, stating that she was pregnant. The man was John Marcos, one of the men she had brought up from Mexico.

Fathering children is a sign of virility in the Hispanic culture, a fact which Diana had counted on. According to Marcos, Diana told him that he was the father of her unborn child. She demanded that he give her money to care for the child, and he didn't object. He listed Diana on his employment medical and life insurance policies, then gave her the money she demanded. Two months later, on October 10, 1983, Diana gave birth to a healthy baby boy in a hospital in Clovis, New Mexico. She named the child Daniel Christopher Marcos.

The deputies had learned from Dr. Allen Pace that a pediatrician in Clovis named Dr. Kyle Mason had treated that baby, so they called Mason and asked him about his history with the child and its mother. The doctor wasn't eager to speak with them, but he said that if they would get a subpoena for copies of the child's records, he would tell them all he knew. They agreed and served the subpoena the following day.

Clovis, New Mexico, is located eight miles west of the Texas border, scarcely more than ten miles from Deputy Bonham's office in Farwell. However, this town lies at the heart of a large farming and commercial center, so it is much larger in size and has broad boulevards lined with fast-food restaurants, gas stations, and small businesses. The deputies found Dr. Mason's office on one of the busy boulevards.

Dr. Mason was a small, frail man with bushy red hair and eyebrows, and a pair of small spectacles perched low on his nose. He had a slight stutter, which became more pronounced as he talked about Diana Lumbrera. He said he remembered her very well, although she had been using the name Diana Marcos in 1983.

Another doctor had delivered the child, Mason

said. Then, because he was a pediatrician, he had been called in that same day to give the child a complete examination. The nursing service informed him that there had been several deaths of children in this family. He said he had found that highly suspicious, so to make certain nothing was wrong with this infant, he had made an exhaustive examination of him, including chest X rays to evaluate the size and shape of his heart.

All of the test results showed that the child was normal and in perfectly good health.

However, Mason's suspicions remained, and fearing that this child might meet the same fate as Diana's other children, he instructed the hospital social worker to visit the infant and his mother, then to contact the state social workers so that the child could be monitored for his own protection. In his "progress notes" from the day of the child's birth, Mason wrote: "I would anticipate that the state social workers would follow the infant for several years."

The following day, he checked the infant and reassured himself that the baby was doing very well. Then he telephoned the hospital social worker to get the results of her interview with Diana and of her call to the state agency.

The woman told him that since it was a holiday, she had decided to do nothing. The doctor's anxiety increased. He knew he had no control over when Diana would be discharged from the hospital, and he was afraid that if she left before a state monitoring system could be established on the child, the opportunity to protect the child would be lost. The social worker promised to make the appropriate arrangements as soon as possible.

But Dr. Mason didn't stop there. When he learned that Diana was planning to move back to Texas, he sat down and wrote a letter to the head of the social service office in Lubbock, asking that medical appointments for the child be coordinated and that protective surveillance of him be carried out in the home.

An entry in his "progress notes" later that same day read: "I have talked to the hospital social worker about this child. [She] is going to call a social worker in Texas and place this child under a protection variety of surveillance. . . . I am going to make an effort to contact the social worker at Texas Tech University and have that social worker supervise the mother's activities in the clinic in the University.

"I have encouraged the hospital social worker, and I will try to have a positive follow-up on this child. The mother tells me that I am not to see the child on follow-up. However, after some difficulty I have acquired the name of a Dr. Allen Pace in Muleshoe who she plans to have the child see in her area. I have told the mother that the child should be seen by Dr. Pace next week. Again, I will try to personally discuss this child's case with Dr. Pace in Muleshoe."

Another entry later that same day read: "I have talked to Dr. Pace about this child. He tells me that he will see this infant if the mother calls him to see the infant. Dr. Pace has been involved in the problems of the children in this family previously. He tells me that this mother has been involved in another unfortunate incident where a young child who was not hers died while in her care."

The entry continued: "I have talked to a social worker in Lubbock at the Health Science Center by the name of Mr. Bob Maher. [He] has agreed to send the Marcos mother an appointment for her child to have the child checked in the pediatric clinic in Texas Tech University College of Medicine. He will also try to see that there is a social service follow-up on this child in the State of Texas."

As the weeks passed, Dr. Mason's anxiety over the child's welfare stayed with him, so at the end of two months he wrote to the same social worker at the Health Science Center in Lubbock.

The letter was dated December 8, 1983, and read: "I referred this family to the center some time back. I would be interested in knowing if the family kept their appointment and what the medical and social findings were."

He received a reply from the social worker one week later, again in the form of a letter. "The family failed to keep a scheduled appointment in the Pediatric Clinic on October 27, 1983. Contact has been made with Carl Meek, Children's Protective Services, Hereford, Texas, in an effort to locate the family.

"Mr. Meek has in turn contacted the Bovina police, however, the family cannot be found. According to Mr. Meek, autopsies performed on the children revealed physiological causes for their deaths. Based on this information his agency has not pursued the matter further being unable to locate the family."

The situation was painfully clear to Dr. Mason. As soon as Diana had learned that her baby was going to be monitored, she moved out of her home without leaving a forwarding address. And because none of the three autopsies that had been performed on her dead children had resulted in suspicious findings, there was no legal obligation for the state agency to pursue the matter further. As far as the local police and the Texas Child Protective Services agency were concerned, the matter was closed.

Three months later, Dr. Mason saw a notice of the child's death in the obituary section of the *Lubbock Avalanche Journal*. It was dated March 29, 1984. The doctor cut it out and pasted it in the child's medical records; it was a grim reminder of a battle lost.

Chapter 18

When the deputies returned to Bonham's office in Farwell, they added Dr. Mason's medical records to the others of Diana and young Christopher that they had already obtained. The picture those records painted was very frightening.

The records showed that shortly after Christopher's birth, Diana apparently cut off all contact with John Marcos, then took the baby to the home of her relative, police lieutenant David Salas, in Dimmitt, Texas. She also made name changes at that time. She changed the baby's name from Daniel Christopher Marcos to Christopher Daniel Lumbrera and her own name from Diana Marcos back to Diana Lumbrera. Those changes were apparently designed to prevent any interested authorities from finding her and her son.

Diana soon rented a small apartment and began going out to bars again, looking for men who would help pay her bills and show her a good time. Her favorite hangout was a large Hispanic bar and dance hall in Dimmitt called *Estrellita,* which means "Little Star" in English. Her behavior there was much the same as it had been in the other bars she had gone to, and she quickly became popular with the men. She gained a reputation for being highly sexual but also dangerous if crossed.

Deputy Jerry Bailey often patrolled the area where Estrellita was located, and he frequently saw Diana partying at the bar with some of her boyfriends. Later in the evening he would sometimes see her having sex in the backseats of various cars which were parked on the old Dump Ground Road. He had even seen her there with more than one man in the same evening.

With Marcos and his money out of the picture, Christopher became an expensive, time-consuming burden on Diana, so it wasn't long before his near-death episodes began. The first occurred on February 8, 1984, when the infant was only four months old. At eleven o'clock that morning, Diana ran into the same tiny medical clinic in Muleshoe where she had gone while still pregnant. She was holding the infant in her arms; he was cyanotic and only semiconscious. She screamed for someone to help her, saying that her baby was sick, then she gave him to the nurse who ran up to help.

She told the nurse that her child had gone into convulsions forty-five minutes earlier and had then passed out. She had rushed him to the emergency room at the nearby hospital, but a doctor wasn't available, so the baby was treated by one of the nurses. Diana said that wasn't good enough for her son, so she had brought him to this clinic, where he would be seen by a doctor.

The deputies would later learn that Diana had not taken the infant to the hospital that day as she had said.

Diana also told the nurse that she had had four children who had previously died: two from "crib death," one from "pneumonia and seizures," and one from "congenital heart failure."

The doctor was summoned and quickly examined the infant. The child soon regained full consciousness, but other than a small cold, nothing appeared to be wrong with him. The doctor was not able to determine what had caused the child to fall into unconsciousness. He prescribed an antibiotic for the child and told Diana to keep a close watch on him. Then he sent the baby home with her.

Diana took the child back to see this same doctor on each of the next two days; each time the doctor reexamined him and reassured her that her child would be all right. It was during one of those visits that Diana told the doctor that she thought she might be pregnant. He administered a test to find out, and it showed that Diana was right. He guessed that she was probably six weeks into the pregnancy at the time. After that visit she never returned to Muleshoe.

Later that month she found work as a nurse's aide at a local nursing home in Dimmitt. Then on March 8, 1984, Diana drove to a small clinic in Lubbock and had an abortion. She apparently thought that she could get rid of Christopher without getting caught but she might not be so lucky with a seventh victim. Too many people were already suspicious of her children's sudden deaths. She asked the doctor for a supply of birth control pills before she left.

Two weeks later Christopher had his next near-death episode. At approximately eight o'clock on the evening of March 20, 1994, Diana ran into the emergency room of the Plains Memorial Hospital in Dimmitt. Five-month-old Christopher was hanging limply in her arms, and she was screaming that her child was sick and for someone to help her.

A nurse ran up to her, and Diana told the woman that Christopher had just had a convulsion and had stopped breathing. The nurse grabbed the child and rushed him into a nearby treatment room. Then Dr. Stan Lenz ran in and began working on the child.

Christopher wasn't quite dead. He was cyanotic, limp, and his eyes were rolled back, but he was still breathing—barely. While the doctor was stabilizing the infant, Diana was outside in the reception area crying and telling the medical staff about her four children who had all tragically died previously.

She seemed to be a hysterical mother who was nearly out of her mind with worry for her young son. She even fainted a number of times. Her audience listened with great sympathy, then did their best to give her their loving support. No one seemed suspicious about the unusual number of deaths.

Dr. Lenz had baby Christopher admitted to the hospital, then ran an exhaustive series of tests on him. The results showed that with the exception of a slight ear infection, the child was normal in every way. He didn't even have a fever. The doctor was unable to determine what had caused the child's condition, so two days later he was released back into Diana's care.

One week later Diana returned to the clinic in Lubbock and obtained another supply of birth control pills. The following day Christopher suddenly and mysteriously died.

The deputies learned that on the morning of March 28, 1984, Diana took Christopher for a car ride with the lieutenant's wife. They returned home a short while later—about nine o'clock.

The wife remembered that Diana had said the baby was sick; however she thought he looked perfectly healthy. Diana's comment had worried the woman, because she knew of the other five children who had died while in Diana's care. The wife would later tell the deputies that she and her police lieutenant husband were becoming suspicious about what had really caused the children's deaths. However, the woman said nothing. She left Diana's house, leaving the child alone with his mother. Half an hour later, a neighbor saw Diana walk out of the house carrying the infant in her arms. She was headed in the direction of the Plains Memorial Hospital, which was two blocks down the street.

Five minutes later Diana walked through the entrance doors of the hospital's emergency room with Christopher's body hanging limply in her arms. She began screaming that he had had a convulsion and had stopped breathing. Then, while Diana put on another show of hysterics and fainting in the reception area, a Code Blue was run on her son.

The child was cyanotic, and the skin was already becoming mottled on the lower portions of his body. He had no heartbeat, no respiration, and he was completely unresponsive. He had obviously been dead for some time. The code lasted ten minutes, then it was stopped and all efforts to save the child ceased.

The doctor in charge of the code was the same doctor who had treated little Christopher only one week earlier, Dr. Stan Lenz. Dr. Lenz decided that the child had probably died from "septicemia," an infection of the blood that affects the entire body. On what Dr. Lenz based his decision, no one will ever know, because his own tests on the child the previous week had shown no blood infection. And after the child was declared dead, no other tests were run.

Most experts think that like SIDS, septicemia is one of those diagnoses that some doctors use when they have no idea what the real cause of death is. It takes them off the hook from having to probe further and ask uncomfortable questions.

Since Dr. Lenz apparently had no suspicions about the death, the justice of the peace was never called and an autopsy was never ordered.

So twenty-five-year-old Diana Lumbrera, a poorly educated, untrained woman with only average intelligence, had just gotten away with her sixth perfect murder. And once again her family and friends poured out their sympathies to her, but no one cried for her tiny victim.

Shortly afterward, Diana moved back into her mother's home in Bovina and went to work at the nearby meat-packing plant. True to her pattern, she worked during the day and partied at night until her mother died in May 1985. Then she moved to Garden City, Kansas, where her younger sister lived. One month later, she was pregnant again.

Chapter 19

Christopher's death looked just like the others. Diana had been alone with him when he stopped breathing, and the real cause of his death had never been determined. The fact that he had ceased to be a money-making device for her was obviously one of her motives, but the deputies wondered if there were more. They began their search of his insurance and burial records, looking for an answer. They soon expanded that search to include records for all the children, then met in Bailey's office to organize the information they had collected.

The two men gathered all the documents and took them to the conference room, where there was a long table they could use. They separated the documents into stacks according to victim, pulled out the amount of insurance coverage, deducted the burial costs, and came up with the amount of money that had been left over after each child had been buried. When they added that information to what they already knew about

Diana and the children's deaths, her probable motives became clearer.

Diana probably murdered her first victim, Joanna, a child she had not wanted, as an act of revenge against her young husband. However, after the child's funeral, the couple received the remaining insurance, $757.50 and a donation from the local Catholic church of about $1,000. The sum of $1,757.50 was big money to the financially strapped seventeen-year-old mother, especially in 1976. That small windfall of cash must have made her consider the act of killing to be yet another way to get money. Such reasoning was consistent with the way she thought.

It also explained why she willingly became pregnant with her third child, José Luís, and why she murdered him less than three months after his birth; she expected to receive another big sum of money after he died. To her disappointment, that didn't happen. The church never took up another collection for the young parents, and the infant's insurance policy was only half the amount of Joanna's. Less than $200 was left after he was buried. Still, as with all the other deaths, José's death did remove the troublesome burden and expense of child care.

Melissa died while Diana and Tony were separated. Her death brought Diana nearly $800 and the freedom to go out partying with her friends every night.

It was with Melinda's death that Diana became so blatantly greedy. She took out the additional life insurance policy less than twelve hours before killing her, then later received $2,523.34 in unspent insurance money after she was buried—more quick cash.

Diana probably didn't kill five-month-old Christopher just for the insurance money, because she knew Christopher's death would bring her less than $200. She had apparently used Christopher to extort money from John Marcos, and once that relationship ended, the child became an unnecessary financial burden. She probably killed Christopher simply because there was no longer any benefit in letting him live.

Finally, the deputies considered the murder of six-week-old Ericka Aleman. Diana knew she wouldn't gain from this child's death, and there was no apparent act of revenge or jealousy involved. What else was left? The two men wondered if Diana had found the act of killing to be exciting. They knew she liked fooling people, because it apparently made her feel powerful and superior. Had the taking of a life given her the ultimate feeling of power? Had she loved the excitement that came from getting away with murder?

The deputies were outraged by the implications of their findings. How could a young mother have been so ruthless, so cunning, and so evil? And how could those in authority ignore the murders of six little children, especially when medical doctors were calling and asking them to investigate?

However, the deputies had a more immediate problem. Diana still hadn't been indicted in any of the Texas counties, and Kansas would be forced to release her any day now. They had to find a way to rush the indictments.

They found very little satisfaction in having answered one of the questions that had troubled them most: If Diana had killed all these children, why hadn't she been caught before now? The answer was simple. She had played the part of a grieving mother in a state legal system where there was too little scrutiny over the deaths of children. It was a system populated with sometimes naive medical and law enforcement officials who refused to believe that parents could cold-bloodedly murder their children, with elected but untrained officials who made the decisions about whether or not autopsies would be performed, with pathologists who were performing forensic autopsies for which they had no training or skill, with insurance officials who were more concerned with the bottom line than with saving children's lives; and with a state Child Protective Services agency that wasn't willing to extend those services to children unless there was clear-cut proof of wrongdoing by the parents. It was a system with little coordination and almost no accountability. And it was a very sad commentary on how things worked in the state of Texas.

Part III

Preparing for Trial

Chapter 20

Diana's attorney was forty-year-old Mike Quint, a married man with five young children at home. Quint was a skilled, tenacious defense attorney, a man with his own distinctive style. He wore a Dutch boy haircut, wire-rimmed glasses and a full beard, and had a folksy manner that charmed witnesses and frequently disarmed his adversaries. He was not the kind of opponent one would take lightly. He and Pierce had been good friends for many years.

The Kansas case had fallen into trouble nearly two weeks earlier, when Quint hired famed forensic pathologist Dr. William G. Eckert to perform a second autopsy on José Lumbrera.

Eckert's credentials were more than impressive. He was internationally recognized as one of the best in his field and had practiced forensic pathology for thirty-five years. The autopsies he had performed numbered between 12,000 and 15,000. He had worked for a coroner's office in Louisiana, run a medical examiner's system in the state of Virginia, and worked at medico-legal and general pathology in the state of Florida. In 1967 he moved to Wichita, Kansas, and made that his home base.

In the years that followed, Dr. Eckert authored numerous forensic text and reference books and worked as a consultant in homicide cases all over the world. Some of those cases included the Robert F. Kennedy assassination, the Charles Manson killings of Sharon Tate and the La Biancas, the John Gacy serial murders, the McMartin Preschool child molestations, the Jonestown massacre in Guyana, South America, the jumbo jet bombing over Lockerbee, Scotland, and the Tenerife plane crash in Spain. He had also worked most of the major homicide cases that had occurred in Kansas. His impressive record earned him the status of a "living legend" in law enforcement circles and made him a well-known figure to those Kansas residents who followed crime stories in newspapers and on television.

Quint had had the child's body disinterred from its grave in Garden City and transported to the Wichita Mortuary Services, a warehouselike building near his home. The next morning, May 18, 1990, Dr. Eckert had begun the child's autopsy.

While this autopsy was under way, Detective James Hawkins was busy digging into the facts of Diana's life in Garden City. He learned that upon arriving she moved in with her sister and soon found work at the Montfort Beef Packing Company. She continued her pattern of working in the daytime and partying in bars at night. She met Juan Martinez, another Montfort worker, in one of those bars and moved into his apartment the following week. She soon became pregnant, but Martinez refused to pay her the money she demanded; he was already supporting a wife and three children in Texas. Diana was nearly seven months pregnant when he came home one night and told her he'd had enough of her crazy behavior; he was moving back to Texas. She was too far along for an abortion, and she had already taken a medical leave of absence from Montfort. She had no way to support herself. She called a coworker, Christina Hernandez, and made a bid for sympathy.

With great emotion, she told Christina that earlier that night someone had broken into her home and had cut her on the stomach with a knife. She said she had already been to the emergency room but had decided against filing a police report. Martinez had been gone all night, and she thought he was probably at a nearby bar.

Unlike Diana, Christina was a kind, loving, devout Catholic who worked hard and lived honestly. She believed Diana and wanted to help. She and her husband found Martinez at the bar and told him about Diana's frantic call. They thought it odd that he didn't seem upset, but it wasn't their business, so they returned home and forgot about the incident. A few days later, Martinez packed up his things and left.

Diana continued to go to Christina for help. She toned down her lifestyle and acted the part of a single mother who had come up on hard times. She never mentioned that she had had five other children or that those children had all suddenly died. Christina let Diana move into her home, where she could take better care of her.

José Antonio was born two months later, and Christina became his godmother, a job she took seriously. When Diana moved into the duplex on Tonio Street, Christina saw the child often, frequently baby-sitting him at night and on weekends. For the next four years Diana lived a double life: to her friends and neighbors, she was the child's loving mother, a role that brought her help with the child and support for herself when she needed it. To the men she met at bars, she was the pretty woman who would party wildly—if they had enough money.

Keeping the two roles separate must have proved difficult, but then, Diana probably knew that it was only a matter of time before the charade would end. If her pattern held true, she would eventually cash in on this child, just as she had on the others.

Later that day Hawkins drove to the Golden Plains Credit Union, to which Diana Lumbrera belonged through her job at Montfort, and spoke with loan officer Joan Steadwell. She was an efficient-looking, dark-haired woman in her mid-thirties who had processed four separate loan applications for Diana Lumbrera.

She said Diana had applied for her first loan on March 30, 1989, thirteen months before José's death. In that application she requested a loan of between $850 and $1,000. Joan interviewed her in person, and she said that José had cancer and was in a hospital in Mexico. He would be getting out soon, so she needed the money to pay his hospital bill.

Joan also had a little boy, and she felt tremendous compassion for Diana. She approved the loan without question and arranged for her to pay the money back through a payroll deduction of $50 per week.

Diana made her second loan application to the credit union five months later, on August 16, 1989. She asked for a loan of $850, and this time Joan interviewed her by telephone. Diana said that her son was returning from Mexico, and she needed the money to purchase a hospital bed and wheelchair for him.

As part of the application, Diana had filled out a current list of all her outstanding debts, and the list was uncomfortably long for a person who earned only $7 an hour. It showed that she owed money to her landlord, to Ford Motor Credit for an automobile, and to the credit union for the unpaid balance of her last loan.

But because repayment would take place through

large monthly payroll deductions and because of the extremely urgent and sad circumstances, Joan approved the loan anyway. She combined the old loan with the new one and arranged to have Diana make payments of $200 per month. Could anyone deny a little boy with cancer the medical equipment he desperately needed?

Eight months later, on April 20, 1990, Diana applied to the credit union for her third loan, making a total of three loans in less than thirteen months. Diana wanted another $850, and once again Joan interviewed her by telephone. Diana said she needed the loan to purchase more hospital equipment for her son. More specifically, the equipment was needed for the blood transfusions that he required.

Joan said Diana's voice had been sad and pitiful as before, but something bothered her about the request. She still felt very sorry for Diana, but an inner sense began to make her doubt that Diana's story was true. She wondered how so much tragedy could befall one person.

Joan went to her supervisor to discuss Diana's request, and the supervisor agreed with the doubts she was having. She told Joan to get the name of the company from which Diana was going to buy the transfusion machine, then to make out a check payable to that company for the exact amount of purchase.

Joan had just returned to her desk when her telephone rang. It was Diana calling again, and this time she was nearly hysterical; she was crying loudly, and she sounded desperate. She told Joan she "needed the money real bad because her father was taking her son to Mexico for another treatment, and they had had a car accident in Arizona and that her father was killed and that her son had broken hips . . . and broken ribs."

Joan was shocked to learn of Diana's latest tragedy. She wondered how Diana managed to handle all her grief, and her heart went out to her. She approved the application immediately, combining the new loan amount with the outstanding balance of the last one. Diana would repay the total loan balance of $1,352.29 by monthly payroll deductions of $240. Then Joan had a check issued to Diana in the amount of $850.

In this last loan application Diana listed her income from Montfort Beef Packing Company as $7.10 per hour. And there was a second source of income listed, the *El Perico Charro* "the Cowboy Parrot." This was a small *tortilla* factory located on the north side of Garden City. Diana wrote that she had been working there during her off-hours since December 1989 for a wage of $3.40 per hour.

Hawkins would later interview the owners of the *tortilla* factory and learn that Diana had, in fact, worked there an average of twenty-five hours a week but had quit after working less than three months. She had omitted that fact on her loan application. So at the time she was applying for the third loan, she knew that with only her Mont-fort salary as income, she wouldn't be able to repay it. She had dug herself into a very deep financial hole, she didn't like working extra hours, and there was no legitimate help in sight. She must have decided that it was time for José to die. It was the only way she had of getting the money she needed.

Ten days later, she ran into the emergency room of St. Catherine's Hospital carrying the body of her dead son in her arms.

Joan told Hawkins that Diana had telephoned her the day after José died. Diana had broken down and sobbed hysterically as she explained that "her son had passed away the night before and that she had life insurance on him but that she might need a loan to pay for some of the burial expenses." Diana had said that "in Texas the funeral homes would not bury her people unless you had the money up front, and she didn't know for sure how it worked in Kansas."

Joan was shocked by the news of the boy's death, and her own emotions quickly over-whelmed her. She cried too. She told Diana to find out what the funeral expenses would be and what the insurance would cover, then to let her know how much money she would need. The fol-lowing day Diana called Joan back and said that she would need $500.

But in spite of Joan's emotional reaction, that inner voice kept nagging at her. She finally listened to it and did absolutely nothing. She didn't issue the check, she didn't call the hospital to verify the boy's death, she didn't call Diana to be convinced that the need for the funeral money was real. She simply set Diana's file on the corner of her desk and waited—for what, she had absolutely no idea. And Diana never called her back.

Hawkins thanked the loan officer and drove back to the LEC. On the way he thought about the implications of what he had just learned. He knew that Diana had lied about needing the $500 to pay for José's funeral. Diana had taken out the $5,000 life insurance policy on the child on April 15, 1989, two weeks after she had applied for her first loan with the credit union. She had needed that $500 to pay overdue bills.

Hawkins thought about the stack of delinquent notices that had been found in Diana's apartment, but Pierce had needed further proof. He needed a person who could take the stand and testify from his or her own personal knowledge about Diana's increasingly desperate financial situation. Presented through such a witness, the information would have a much greater impact on the jury than if it were presented by a detective reading off the stack of bills he had found.

Hawkins was sure that Joan Steadwell was just that witness. With her testimony, the prosecutor could argue that Diana had murdered her little boy because she had needed him dead more than she had wanted him alive.

Hawkins returned to his office just before lunch and telephoned Pierce. The prosecutor was ecstatic when he heard what Hawkins had learned.

Two blocks down the street Mike Quint was receiving another telephone call, from Dr. William Eckert, with the results of his autopsy on José Antonio Lumbrera.

Chapter 21

Everyone attending the attorneys' luncheon had been served, but Ricklin Pierce was much too upset to eat. He sat at the table, pushing food around on his plate, trying to convince himself that Quint had been joking. He desperately wanted to leave, but he knew it wouldn't be polite, and he prayed that the guest speaker would hurry up and sit down. When the break came, he left through a side exit and raced back to the LEC. He found Elliott and Hawkins at their desks somberly discussing the case.

The detectives told him that they had just received a call from Kansas Bureau of Investigation (KBI) agent Ed Bartkowski. Bartkowski had attended the child's autopsy, and he had informed them of Eckert's findings—death from natural causes.

He said Eckert's external examination of the body revealed three circular bruises approximately three-quarters of an inch in diameter on the child's right thigh and below his right knee. They appeared to be bruises left by the finger pressure of an adult. (Those bruises had not been mentioned on the autopsy report made by Dr. Eva Vachal two weeks earlier.)

His internal examination of the body and skeleton revealed no evidence of past abuse, that is, no old bruises or fractured bones, which proved that José had not been severely beaten during his lifetime.

Eckert had had a copy of Dr. Vachal's preliminary autopsy report, and he made mention of some of her observations, such as the condition of the larynx. She had kept the larynx, along with some of the child's other organs, at St. Catherine's, and in her preliminary report she had stated that it showed no signs of injury. An uninjured larynx meant that the child had not been strangled.

She had also mentioned the petechiae on the child's face, the linear hemorrhage in the conjunctiva of his right eye, and the hemorrhage in his lungs. And although Dr. Eckert had also made mention of these, he did not agree with her conclusions. He felt that an infection of the gastrointestinal tract, not smothering, had brought about the child's death.

Eckert would later send his preliminary report to Mike Quint, and in it he would write that he would still "have to look at the microscopics of the lung and hear of the result of the toxicology to give [his final] opinion."

However, in a cover letter he would write: "I can see no evidence that this is anything but a natural death. Smothering would be evident if we were to find signs of pressure of manual or instrumental nature. I did not see any signs of any sort of external injury. I saw no marks on the nostrils or fibers inside the nasal cavity.

"In view of the fact that José was ill the day before he died, the worsening of his illness could have occurred. I cannot give any opinion at this point that this was a death by unnatural causes unless the toxicology shows some evidence of poisoning.

"I would be happy to consult with the Prosecutor in this as he should be brought abreast of the problems presented by this case."

Pierce listened to the detectives but said nothing. He couldn't believe this had happened. He knew Quint had hired Eckert to perform a second autopsy, but he had expected Eckert's results to support those of Dr. Eva Vachal, not to directly oppose them. At worst, he had thought that Eckert might label the cause of death as "undetermined." But never this!

He flopped down in a chair next to one of the desks and sat there in silence, his confidence badly shaken. Finally, he got up, thanked the detectives, and walked slowly back to the courthouse. He had to have time to think.

The inexperienced prosecutor didn't question Dr. Eckert's competency. He had seen the man's outstanding work firsthand and had heard the wonderful tales of the KBI agents and local detectives who had used the famous doctor on their cases. Everyone knew that Eckert was a man whose work was beyond question.

Instead, Pierce questioned his own judgment. Self-doubts flooded his mind as he struggled to figure out where he had gone wrong. Had he made a tremendous error in judgment? After all, this was his first murder case. Had he been blinded by the fact that six other children had died while in Diana Lumbrera's care? Had he falsely accused this woman of the murder of her own child? Finally he took out the Lumbrera file and reread the police and medical reports one more time. But still none of it made sense unless one first accepted Dr. Vachal's conclusions.

He decided to focus on something else and was going through the papers in his in-basket when he came across a large manila envelope. He opened it and found copies of police reports written by Texas deputies Bailey and Bonham and forwarded to him by Detective Hawkins.

The reports detailed the conversations the deputies had had with Drs. Purdy and Mason. They told of the two doctors' suspicions and how they had both contacted the state agencies in Texas in an effort to protect Diana's remaining children. They described how an enraged Dr. Purdy had even contacted the local sheriff to get an investigation started into the children's deaths. Yet nobody had listened, and nothing had been done, so more children had eventually died.

Pierce's frustration with Eckert's autopsy made him want to scream. Instead, he threw the reports back in the basket, grabbed his coat, and went home. He knew there had to be something he could do—if only he could figure out what.

On Friday, when Quint had told Pierce about Eckert's autopsy findings, he had also pointed out that the state no longer had a case against Diana Lumbrera. By Monday that information had leaked to newspaper and television reporters in Wichita and Garden City.

In Wichita, reporters interviewed Dr. Eckert, while their colleagues in Garden City asked their own questions of Mike Quint. By five o'clock that afternoon the entire story of Diana Lumbrera's tragic loss of six children, her sudden arrest and incarceration, and then Dr. Eckert's evidence of her innocence had gone nationwide.

In the afternoon edition of the *Garden City Telegram*, a bold front page headline read, SECOND AUTOPSY: 'NATURAL CAUSES.' The reporter quoted Quint as saying that he would go into court the following day and ask that his client, Diana Lumbrera, who was being held in jail on a $50,000 bond, be released on a personal recognizance bond—that is, that she be released on only her promise to appear at her next court hearing.

Quint was also quoted as saying that he didn't know if Ricklin Pierce would pursue the murder charge against Lumbrera but that his [Pierce's] decision would probably be based on Dr. Eckert's final autopsy results, which would soon be available. The article then went on to requote those individuals who had always thought Diana innocent of the murder charge.

The reporter had even called Texas prosecutor Johnny Actkinson and informed him of Dr. Eckert's findings. A week earlier Actkinson had told the reporter that he had three baskets on his desk. "One of them is for evidence that shows she [Diana] intentionally did this. We don't have anything in that basket. We have another basket that's getting pretty full of evidence that would tend to show that, while maybe not abusive, she was an extremely neglectful parent. These children were not well taken care of. Our third basket is that all of the deaths were coincidental. And it just seems to be too many deaths to be that." But learning of Dr. Eckert's findings put even more doubt about Diana's guilt in Actkinson's mind. He told the reporter he was not prepared to suggest any wrongdoing, then added that it was only a routine police investigation.

The reporter's story ended with a statement that Ricklin Pierce had been in court during the time the news release was being prepared and could not be reached for comment.

When Pierce heard about Quint's conversation with the press, he dropped everything and raced over to the LEC to meet with the detectives. He was angry and frightened, and he needed to talk strategy, to make sure there were no more surprises coming their way. The two detectives were just coming out of Captain Armentrout's office when Pierce ran in.

While the two men listened, Pierce paced up and

down the narrow aisle between their desks and talked at length. He talked about the two autopsies, the press reports that would be coming out that afternoon, and Quint's intention to get Diana released without posting a bond. Pierce was tired and upset, and the detectives could see the fear in his face.

Pierce had a good reason for being afraid. He was sure that if Quint was successful, Diana would be gone from Garden City before nightfall. He was also sure that if she did leave, they'd never find her.

And even if the Kansas case was lost, Pierce was certain that the Texas investigation would lead to one or more convictions. He'd been getting copies of the reports Deputy Jerry Bailey had been sending almost daily from Texas, and the Texas investigation was finally falling into place.

So how would he feel, how would they all feel, if Diana disappeared before Texas had the legal authority to take her into custody?

When Ken Elliott arrived at work the next morning he was filled with anxiety, but he had an idea. He thought Quint and the press might have misunderstood Eckert's autopsy results, so he poured himself some coffee, placed a call to Wichita Mortuary Services, and asked to speak directly to Dr. Eckert. Eckert wasn't there. Elliott then tried the doctor's home, which he had done during other murder investigations. The doctor's wife answered and called her husband to the phone.

"Hello, Dr. Eckert. This is Detective Elliott with

Garden City Police Department." Elliott kept his voice friendly with no hint of anxiety. "I'd like to talk to you about the re-autopsy you did on José Lumbrera and discuss the cause of death you came up with on the child."

The famous pathologist remembered Elliott and was agreeable. He began to explain about the findings of his autopsy, but his explanation was rushed and filled with complicated medical terminology that the detective had a hard time following. The doctor summed up his findings by saying simply that the child had died from a gastrointestinal-tract infection.

Like other investigators who had worked with Eckert, Elliott had tremendous respect for him. He knew how much Eckert loved to teach and how he would always go into great detail when asked about some particular aspect of his work. So Elliott asked him questions about why he had ruled out smothering and how he had reached his conclusion that the child had died from an infection.

But this time the doctor's reaction to Elliott's questions was markedly different than it had been on earlier occasions. In fact, Elliott found it so out of character that he mentioned it at the end of the supplemental report he wrote immediately afterward. "Dr. Eckert reminded me that he was being employed by Michael Quint, the suspect's attorney."

Elliott was troubled by the strange conversation, so he discussed it first with Armentrout, then he telephoned Pierce. Pierce walked to the LEC to have Elliott go over it again. The prosecutor had no reaction until the detective repeated Eckert's comment about being employed by Michael Quint. Then a funny expression slowly crossed Pierce's face and his mouth fell open. "So that's it," he mumbled to himself. "He's a hired gun!"

Pierce became animated with excitement. He told the detectives to find out who was the top forensic pathologist in the nation and get him or her to review the autopsy data. If that expert agreed with Eckert, he would drop all charges against Diana Lumbrera and end the investigation. But if he or she agreed with Eva Vachal, he would prosecute Diana to the hilt. He had no intention of letting the case end here.

Chapter 22

Pierce and Quint stood looking up at Judge Stephen Nyswonger in the main courtroom. Diana sat by herself at the defense table, nervously bouncing a pencil in her right hand. Nyswonger was a handsome man in his early fifties with broad shoulders, curly dark hair, and bifocal glasses. A surly look was just beginning to form on his face as he listened to Mike Quint explain why Diana should be released on personal recognizance. Pierce was quietly waiting his turn and trying his best not to look desperate.

Quint argued that since Eckert's findings, which clearly carried more weight than those of Dr. Vachal, indicated that the boy's death had been from natural causes, then in all probability Diana was innocent. Therefore, forcing his client to stay in jail because of an unnecessarily high bail was creating an undue hardship on her; she was, after all, just a grieving young mother.

When Quint finished, Pierce countered passionately, saying he had considerable evidence that showed the child had been murdered by the defendant. He pleaded with the judge to keep Diana in jail until he had the chance to present that evidence.

Judge Nyswonger was not impressed by medical resumes, so he left Diana's bail at $50,000 and told the two men they could fight it out at the preliminary hearing, scheduled to be held in less than twenty days.

But Pierce wanted more. He wanted the judge to stop Quint from taking his case to the press, especially before the prelim was held. Quint strongly objected, but the judge agreed. He said the news coverage was injurious to Diana's right to receive a fair trial and strongly suggested that communications with the press be stopped immediately. The judge's suggestion wasn't an official gag order, but it carried almost the same weight.

Pierce hadn't reckoned with the fury of a reporter scorned, however. The next day a blistering editorial appeared in the local newspaper, written by the person who had been covering this case from the start. The man had become livid when he learned what had happened at the hearing, and he accused Pierce of trying to gag the news. He referred to him as a gunslinging, trigger-happy prosecutor.

As Pierce read the editorial, he reminded himself of the source of that criticism, a reporter who he thought was much too fond of the limelight and someone he'd never liked anyway. Then he tossed the newspaper in the trash.

He had managed to buy the Texas authorities a

little time, so the next step was bolstering his own case.

Several days passed before Pierce got his first lead. He slammed down the phone, raced out of his office, and headed for St. Catherine's Hospital. Dr. Eva Vachal had a book written by a forensic pathologist who might be perfect for this case. The pathologist was Dr. Michael Baden, and his book was titled *Unnatural Death: Confessions of a Medical Examiner.*

Dr. Vachal told Pierce she had spent the morning reading a book by Dr. William Eckert. In fact, her desk was piled high with copies of all his books and medical articles, which she had been reviewing in an attempt to understand the man's background and expertise. What was bothering her was that in the days preceding Eckert's re-autopsy, she had telephoned him several times to offer whatever organs or tissue slides he would need for the procedure. Eckert had taken her first call, and they had chatted briefly, but after that he had refused to talk to her or return her calls. She sent him the tissue slides anyway.

After learning of his autopsy results, she had telephoned him again, this time to find out what she had missed or what he had found that resulted in such a different diagnosis. But, as before, Eckert refused to call her back. She didn't understand why.

Pierce thought he knew. He gave Eva Vachal firm instructions to cooperate fully with any requests from Dr. Eckert but to stop trying to contact him or volunteer anything.

Dr. Vachal agreed, but she was still bothered by Eckert's strange behavior. Scientists worked together to solve problems, and his refusal to talk to her went against the grain.

Later that day Pierce would give the same directive to Elliott and Hawkins. He had no idea how important those instructions would later prove to be.

Dr. Vachal handed Pierce the book *Unnatural Death*, which Baden wrote with journalist Judith Adler Hennessee, then told him about Baden's background. He was executive director of the Forensic Sciences Consultant Unit of the New York State Police, which provided forensic services to the sixty-three counties of New York state. He had worked as a medical examiner for the City of New York, one of the largest coroner's offices in the United States, for twenty-five years, including serving as its chief medical examiner.

During that time he had personally performed well over 20,000 medico-legal autopsies, and more than 50 of those autopsies had involved victims of smothering. Not surprisingly, he had testified in criminal and civil cases all over the United States. Like Eckert, Baden had written numerous books and professional articles and had also performed autopsies on some of the rich and famous, including actor/comedian John Belushi and socialite Sunny von Bülow. He had also headed the congressional Select Committee on Assassination medical investigation into the deaths of Reverend Martin Luther

King, Jr., and President John F. Kennedy. Baden would later serve as part of the O.J. Simpson defense team.

The book Dr. Vachal handed Pierce chronicled a series of death investigations that had occurred in upstate New York over a fourteen-year period. The chapter titled "Crazy Quilt" discussed serial killers and included an investigation into the deaths of nine infants belonging to a woman named Mary Beth Tinning. The circumstances in those deaths and those in the deaths of the seven children who were in Diana Lumbrera's care were amazingly similar.

Mary Beth Tinning was a housewife who lived with her husband, Joseph, in a nice middle-class neighborhood. In the thirteen-year period between 1972 and 1985, Mrs. Tinning had given birth to eight children and had adopted one other. All nine children died suddenly and mysteriously while the mother was alone with them, but no one became openly suspicious until after the ninth child had died.

In his book, Dr. Baden examined the question of whether Mrs. Tinning had murdered eight of her children, and if so, how she had gotten away with it for so long. He believed the primary reason had to do with the belief system of the doctors who had determined the cause of each child's death. In essence, the idea that a parent could intentionally kill her child was so repugnant to all of them that they refused even to consider it. It was more comfortable to live in denial and give "wastebasket diagnoses" as the causes of the children's deaths. Dr. Baden defined a wastebasket diagnosis as a diagnosis made in the absence of any true findings.

It was after the ninth death that Dr. Baden was asked to review all of the deaths of the Tinning children to determine if any had been the result of homicide. When he looked at all the Tinning records, he was amazed that none of the deaths had ever been investigated.

In his book he wrote: "Each death by itself could have been explained away innocently, but not if it was viewed as part of a cluster. . . . The police had been utterly incurious—not only had they not questioned Mary Beth and Joseph Tinning, they had never interviewed their neighbors, friends, or family. The social workers who were sent in lieu of the police found no evidence of child abuse or neglect; there was none to find."

According to Dr. Baden, his role as medical examiner was to "confirm the victims—that is, to certify that they *were* victims of a particular killer and to find the pattern." And he did find that pattern.

Mary Beth Tinning had repeatedly run into the hospital emergency room with a dead or near-dead baby in her arms. Each time the child had been cyanotic and not breathing (or barely breathing). And each time she had been the only one present when that child had stopped breathing. She would sometimes tell the doctors that the child had experienced a seizure sometime earlier—again, when she was alone with it. But the doctors would never see any of the children experience such seizures.

The next thing Dr. Baden did was to rule out the causes of death as listed on the death certificates. In each case he found that the stated cause did not fit the medical facts. All of them were simply convenient labels that had been used at the time to avoid having to deal with any darker possibilities.

Mary Beth Tinning was later charged with the first-degree murder of her last child, Tami Lynne, and tried for that crime in 1987. The jury found her guilty of second-degree murder, a lesser offense, and she was sentenced to twenty-five years to life. And even though she would serve only a portion of that sentence, the prosecutor decided not to try her for the deaths of any of the other eight children. He felt he didn't have sufficient evidence to prove that she had also murdered them.

As Dr. Baden concluded the section in his book that covered the Tinning investigation, he made some very interesting points. He talked about the role that social workers play in circumstances of this sort.

"Social workers have a conceptual problem with this kind of tragedy. They assume their role is to be an advocate for the bereaved family, not the children. After every death they came to comfort [Mrs.] Tinning, who thrived on the attention. Instead of being questioned by the police, she got sympathy from the social workers. The doctors were equally sympathetic, as were her family, friends, and neighbors. All the death certificates reported natural causes. Nobody wanted to ask hard questions. Tinning became a sympathy junkie. She was the woman who lost babies."

Dr. Baden also talked about suffocation. He said, "Smothering infants . . . is a repetitive crime. It is one of the few homicides that is repetitive, along with child battery and rape/murders."

Those last words of Baden's mirrored Pierce's own thoughts. He had already guessed that in order to ensure a conviction, he would need to show that José's death was simply the seventh and last in his mother's fourteen-year killing spree. He was sure that if the jury could see the whole picture, they would conclude that this woman had simply killed another child. He had to find a way to get that information before the jury.

When Pierce stopped by the LEC early Monday morning to talk to the detectives, he received his next unexpected piece of good luck. Captain Armentrout handed him a plain envelope mailed anonymously from somewhere in Texas with no return address. It contained a paperback book titled *From Cradle to Grave*, by Joyce Egginton.

The book chronicled the murders of Mary Beth Tinning's eight children, the subsequent police investigation, and the murder trial that had ended in her single conviction. It also mentioned Dr. Baden's involvement in the case and described a mental illness called Munchausen syndrome by proxy, a psychiatric term for "sympathy junkie."

Munchausen Syndrome is a mental illness which causes people to harm themselves in order to gain sympathy or attention. The illness was first described in the medical literature in 1977, and was named after Baron Karl F. H. von Munchausen, an eighteenth-century German cavalry officer who returned home from war against the Turks and told embellished tales of his adventures.

Munchausen syndrome by proxy (MSBP) is a mental illness that causes a person to hurt her children for the attention it brings to herself. The typical MSBP parent is a mother between the ages of twenty-five and forty, often with a health care background. The victims of these parents are mostly infants and toddlers, children who are too young to talk. They are not injured during an ugly outburst of rage by the parent. They are made ill, often deathly ill, through carefully designed intentional acts, then rushed to a doctor before dying. The apparently distraught parent basks in the sympathetic attention provided by a compassionate medical staff while their colleagues work frantically to save the child's life. When one child becomes old enough to talk, the parent will begin practicing her sick methods on a younger sibling.

However, MSBP parents do not typically murder their victims; that would be like killing the goose that lays the golden eggs. They need the child to stay alive so that they can repeat the attention-getting behavior over and over again. They are addicted to the attention that the behavior brings. This is where Mary Beth Tinning differed from the norm. Mary Beth had what is called Fatal MSBP, because she was willing to kill to get the extra attention brought by her child's death.

The gift of the book from the anonymous donor in Texas was amazingly timely, and when Pierce returned to his office, he closed his door and read it completely through.

It was early afternoon when he finished, and as he put the book down, a wave of disappointment swept over him. MSBP didn't fit as a motive for the Lumbrera murders. The Texas reports showed that Diana hadn't made frequent visits to the emergency wards with her children. And when they did survive a trip to the hospital, it was either because she was setting them up to be killed days later or she had just botched an attempt to kill them right then. Plus three of her children lived well past their infancy; the oldest was over four years old. And although Diana obviously enjoyed performing for attention, that wasn't the reason she had murdered the seven children. She had murdered them for money, pleasure, revenge, or just to get rid of them. Diana wasn't sick; she was evil.

The prosecutor thought that a conservative jury might reluctantly accept mental illness as a reason for a mother murdering her child. But for money? Not likely. How would he ever convince them that this woman, an apparently respectable, hardworking single parent, had cruelly murdered her little boy to get her hands on $2,000? He hoped Dr. Baden would be able to help.

* * *

Monday afternoon Hawkins contacted Dr. Baden. There was no pretentiousness in the doctor's manner, and he seemed very interested in the case. He told Hawkins to send him the existing documentation for all seven children, and he would search for Diana's pattern.

Hawkins appreciated the doctor's willingness to help, but he didn't feel comfortable mentioning that the prelim was less than two weeks away and that his findings might be needed in order to keep Diana in custody. Baden was obviously a busy man, and the detective felt lucky just to have his help—in any time frame.

Meanwhile, Elliott was lining up a second expert witness. He had learned from the Finney County Sheriff's Department of an institution in Denver called the C. Henry Kempe National Center for the Prevention of Child Abuse and Neglect. Made up of highly trained individuals, the center was part of the Pediatrics Department of the University of Colorado School of Medicine. Its founder, Dr. C. Henry Kempe, had been one of the early clinical researchers on the issues of child abuse and neglect, and it was he who coined the term "the battered child syndrome."

In 1972, the center had begun serving as a nationwide resource, using a team of experts from various disciplines to review cases sent to it. This team approach enabled the center to quickly identify cases where serious crimes against children had occurred and to locate appropriate experts to assist investigators.

Elliott was told to submit a letter requesting the center's help, along with copies of all existing documentation, including medical reports, police reports, a history of the victims and the suspect, and a list of all law enforcement and medical personnel involved in the investigation.

The detective put a great deal of effort into writing a convincing letter. He described the victim, the circumstances surrounding the Code Blue, and the conflicting results of the two autopsies, and included a short summary of the deaths of the other six children who had died so suddenly while in Diana's care.

Then he asked the center to answer three questions: (1) Is the cause of death consistent with smothering, and if so, how? (2) How much physical evidence would have disappeared between the two autopsies due to the time and/or embalming of the body? (3) How could a child this age be smothered without causing external signs of trauma?

Unlike Hawkins, Elliott ended his request on an urgent note. He informed the center that the Lumbrera case had been set for preliminary hearing on June 12, 1990. This gave the center staff less than ten days to review all of the data and get their findings back to Garden City, if they decided to help in the first place.

It wasn't much time for such a large request, and that fact worried Elliott a great deal. He finished the letter, tucked it and the documents into an Express Mail envelope, and hurried to the post office.

Texas was busy lining up its own forensic pathology expert. Ranger Yeager had learned of Pierce's strategy and had agreed that it was an excellent idea, but his choice of experts had been Dr. Robert Bux, a forty-two-year-old forensic pathologist who worked for the Bexar (pronounced "Bear") County Medical Examiner's Office in San Antonio. The Texas Rangers had used Bux before because his work was thorough, he was effective on the witness stand, and he had a unique tell-it-like-it-is approach that appealed to them. Bux didn't have to be talked into investigating a possible baby killer; he quickly agreed to review the six Texas deaths.

For Pierce and all the lawmen, the entry of these experts into the Lumbrera investigations represented a turning point, and for the first time in a week they began to feel hopeful again. Now they could only hope that the preliminary hearing would keep Diana behind bars.

The morning of Tuesday, June 12, 1990, was cold and gray in Garden City, Kansas. Detective Ken Elliott stared out a window of the LEC, his mood as gloomy as the weather outside. They had all worked so hard to put this case together, and soon it might all be lost.

Diana Lumbrera's preliminary hearing would be starting in a few minutes, but neither Baden nor the Kempe Center had yet reached any conclusions about the seven deaths. They needed more time. There would be no forensic experts coming to the rescue of Dr. Eva Vachal. Even worse, Texas still hadn't indicted Diana for any of the murders in that state. Once the hearing was over, the officers would have no way to legally detain her.

That meant it was all up to Richard Hodson, the assistant prosecutor who had been assigned to handle Diana's prelim. Hodson had never handled a murder case before—not even at the prelim level. Elliott knew that the long-established procedure in the county attorney's office was for an assistant prosecutor to handle the prelim, then the county attorney himself would handle the trial. Elliott thought it was a stupid way to run things, but then Pierce hadn't had any choice; he had been bound by his predecessor's system. So, an inexperienced assistant prosecutor would soon be going into the hearing with very little ammunition to use against the famous Dr. William Eckert.

Pierce was in the main courtroom of the Finney County Courthouse down the street. He was occupied with an unrelated felony trial, about to begin its final day of testimony. He was edgy about Diana's prelim, and he hoped the trial would end early so that he could go over and see how Hodson was doing.

Richard Hodson was in his office upstairs in the courthouse, nervously organizing his notes and the exhibits he planned to introduce when he presented his case. Hodson was a heavyset man in his midforties with thick, wavy brown hair, metal-rimmed glasses, and a mind-set that always kept him tightly controlled. At ten minutes before nine o'clock he carefully packed up his materials, brushed any remaining lint off his dark, double-breasted suit, and headed for the basement courtroom of the LEC.

The courtroom was humming with activity. Reporters had come early to secure good places, while their camera crews took up positions along the side walls. The remaining seats had been filled by curious spectators, Diana's sister, Isabel, and a few of her friends. A group of latecomers stood unhappily near the door, trying to decide whether to stay and stand.

Hodson moved through the crowd and took his seat at the prosecution's counsel table. He removed the materials from his briefcase, organized them neatly on the table in front of him, then focused his attention on his notes. He did his best to ignore everything else around him.

He was under a great deal of pressure. The Lumbrera case had been receiving constant attention in the local and state media, and now even national news organizations were following it. If he lost this one, his reputation as a prosecutor would be damaged for a long time to come.

He looked up as Mike Quint and Diana Lumbrera walked into the room and took their seats at the other counsel table. Quint looked relaxed and confident in his dark blue suit and starched shirt, a fact that only made Hodson more nervous.

Quint had good reason to feel confident; the famous Dr. Eckert was waiting out in the hallway. Quint put his hand on Diana's shoulder and reassured her that everything would be fine. Her case would soon be over, and she'd be free to return to her own life.

As Diana listened to her attorney, the growing number of curious spectators, reporters, and camera crews were watching her every move. She was wearing a tight black dress that her sister had brought her, and fresh makeup, which she had applied carefully an hour earlier. She looked like an attractive, well-kept young mother—certainly not the kind of person who would murder a child. Some of those watching her sensed that she was enjoying being the center of attention.

By nine o'clock, the courtroom was filled with so much nervous tension that everyone was slightly startled when magistrate judge Claude S. Heath III, entered suddenly from a door behind the judge's bench. All present quickly rose to their feet and stood silently until he had stepped onto the platform and seated himself in the oversized black leather chair. Then everyone sat down, and the hearing began.

Judge Heath was a short, thin man with a full head of curly blond hair and a well-trimmed blond beard. He wore a business suit and held a sheath of papers in his right hand. He was not one to waste words, so he got down to business immediately.

"Let the record show this is Case Number 90 CR 222, and it's entitled *State of Kansas* versus *Lumbrera*," he announced loudly as he read from the papers in front of him. Then looking down at the persons occupying the counsel tables, he continued, "The defendant is present in person and is represented by her attorney, Mr. Michael Quint. The State is represented by the Assistant County Attorney for Finney County, Kansas, Mr. Richard Hodson."

Judge Heath first addressed any concerns held by the attorneys, and both attorneys asked that the cameras be barred from the hearing. The judge refused to make them leave, then Hodson began to present his case.

Richard Hodson had to convince the judge of two things: first, that José *probably* had been murdered, and second, that Diana *probably* had been the one who had murdered him. He hoped to prove the first point through the testimony of the doctors who had worked on the child around the time of his death.

His first witness was Dr. Albert H. Gaines, the emergency room physician who had treated José the night of April 30. Dr. Gaines described the tests he had performed on the child and their results, which showed that the child had suffered from a mild respiratory infection—certainly nothing life-threatening.

Gaines also testified about the four vials of amoxicillin that had been given to Diana that night. Detective Utz would later testify about finding the unopened vials in Diana's refrigerator.

Hodson next called Dr. Michael Shull and had him describe the events of the Code Blue that had been run on José the night of May 1. The doctor included seeing the petechiae, whose presence he couldn't explain because there had been no obstructions in the child's airways, no indication of vomiting, and no indication of an infection strong enough to damage the capillary walls.

Diana showed no interest in what the doctors were saying. In fact, she seemed totally indifferent to what was going on around her. The only expression one could detect on her face was boredom. She glanced out the window or played with a button on the front of her black dress as the witnesses talked.

In the week preceding the prelim, Drs. Shull and Vachal had given Hodson the idea he needed to develop his strategy for this hearing. It was based on the concept of an "organ system failure," and he brought it out first with Shull. He asked if it was possible for a person to die from a massive infection, as Eckert's autopsy had found, and if so, how that infection could lead to death.

Shull said that the degree of infection would have to be so great that it would cause an "organ system failure," such as the failure of the respiratory system (lungs), or cardiac system (heart), or digestive system (stomach), etc. He said it would be the failure of that system that would actually cause the death.

Hodson kept his questions short and focused, and soon Shull was excused and the hearing recessed for the normal lunch break.

The hearing resumed at one-thirty, and once again Diana sat quietly at the counsel table with a look of complete indifference on her face. Hodson called Dr. Lauren Welch, the other doctor who had worked José Lumbrera's Code Blue.

Welch's testimony supported that already given by Shull, and added information on the petechiae.

He said he had seen petechiae on patients who had died from tremendous pressure to the body or massive infections, and the pattern of their petechiae was always generalized over the entire body. However, the pattern on José had been different. It had been concentrated around his face and neck, such as would be seen if pressure had been applied just to his face.

The doctor's testimony was long, and frequent objections by Quint strung it out even longer. By the time Welch was excused, it was nearly two-thirty. Hodson then called his prime witness, Dr. Eva Vachal, to the stand.

Most of Hodson's argument was based on the testimony that Dr. Vachal would give. He knew that if she did poorly and failed to convince the judge that her findings could be trusted, the case was over. He also knew that she had very little experience in giving trial testimony. He had to work hard to keep his nervousness from showing as she walked into the room.

Eva Vachal wore a conservative brown business suit and looked more like a college professor than someone who spent most of her time in a laboratory dissecting dead bodies.

As Dr. Vachal was sworn in, Diana Lumbrera stood up and was led out of the courtroom by a deputy sheriff. Quint had gotten permission for Diana to leave because he didn't want her present when they discussed José's autopsy or passed around the gruesome photographs that had been taken during that procedure. Nor did he want the photographers taking any pictures of her during such a discussion. So far she had shown absolutely no emotion, which was worrying him a great deal, and he didn't want anyone getting the idea that she had no feelings for her dead child.

Dr. Vachal hated having to testify in front of a crowd of people, but more than anything, she hated being pitted against Dr. William G. Eckert, a man whose skill as a courtroom witness was legendary. There were two things at stake here: keeping a baby killer off the street and saving her own career. In opposing the famous doctor's findings, she had put her career on the line. The "old boy network" ran deep in the field of pathology, and if her findings weren't accepted, it would forever damage her credibility. She tried not to think about Eckert, concentrating her attention on Richard Hodson instead.

Hodson began by asking the doctor about her qualifications in order to establish her credibility as a witness. When she answered her voice was so soft and quiet that he had to ask her to repeat herself. She started again, briefly describing her education and experience. She said she had been a practicing general pathologist for sixteen years. During that period of time she had performed approximately five hundred autopsies, perhaps two hundred of them on children.

Hodson then had her describe the circumstances surrounding the autopsy of four-year-old José Lumbrera.

Dr. Vachal explained that prior to the autopsy, Dr. Shull had met with her to describe the child's

Code Blue and the fact that his mother had had five other children who had died. So, during her autopsy she had been especially careful to check for the possibility of genetic defects that might have caused the child's death. Then she discussed the findings of her external examination of the child's body, specifically the petechiae on his face and neck and the linear hemorrhage in his right eye.

"Doctor, based on your education, your training, and your experience as of the morning of May 2, when you first viewed the body of José Lumbrera, had you been taught or educated or trained to associate this combination of physical symptoms with any particular medical cause . . .?"

"Yes."

"And what cause was that?"

"Asphyxia," she said firmly.

Hodson had the doctor explain how a person's heart rate would accelerate when air to the lungs was cut off and how this would cause the pressure in the vascular system to increase to the point of causing petechial ruptures in the thin skin on the person's face and neck.

Next she gave her findings from the internal examination of the child's body by describing the condition of each organ. All the child's organs had been completely normal.

Hodson continued his examination of Dr. Eva Vachal for some time, and she consistently gave thorough and detailed explanations to each of his questions. He again employed his strategy of an organ system failure.

He asked if a massive viral or bacterial infection could lead to a person's death, and like Dr. Shull, she said the infection would lead to the failure of at least one organ system. It would be the failure of that system or systems that would actually cause the death.

Hodson wanted to know what symptoms a person would have exhibited prior to his death if his death had been the result of such an organ system shutdown.

Dr. Vachal took each system one by one and explained the specific symptoms that one would expect to find. José's medical records showed that he had not demonstrated any of those symptoms. Finally, Hodson came to the critical questions.

'In the conduct of your autopsy, did you find any evidence at all to indicate or to support a diagnosis of death by natural causes?"

"No," she said flatly.

"Any evidence to support a diagnosis of death due to illness?"

"No."

"And what did you conclude as the cause of death?"

"That the cause of death was asphyxia due to smothering."

After a few more questions regarding the research she had done to confirm her findings of death by smothering, Hodson was finished with her. He was sure that she had done a good job, and he hoped the judge felt the same way.

Mike Quint went on the offensive, drilling Dr.

Vachal on the specifics of her findings and on other possible explanations for what she had found. She never wavered from her belief about what had caused José's death, and she was on the witness stand nearly two hours before she was finally excused. The judge called a short recess.

When the hearing resumed, Quint asked that Dr. Eckert be allowed to testify next, which was out of the usual order. He explained that the doctor needed to return to Wichita that evening and that making him stay in Garden City another day or two would be an undue hardship on the busy pathologist. No one argued the point, and he was called to the stand.

Dr. Eckert was short and round with a thinning crown of graying blond hair and plastic-rimmed eyeglasses. He had a peculiar habit of turning his head first, then following that motion with his body. He raised his hand and was sworn in, then he sat down and waited confidently for Quint to begin.

Normally, Quint would have waited until the trial to have his key witness testify, but he had an important reason for having him testify at this hearing. He knew Eckert was past retirement age and that he had already suffered at least one small stroke. He was worried that the doctor might have another stroke or, even worse, a heart attack before the trial was held—if the case ever went to trial. Quint wanted to make sure that Eckert's own testimony about his autopsy findings had been given at the prelim. That way it could be read at the trial if he was not physically able to be there in person.

Quint had the famous doctor give a résumé of his education, training, and experience, then explain the difference between the education and training of a general pathologist, like Dr. Eva Vachal, and that of a forensic pathologist, like the doctor himself.

Dr. Eckert explained about the additional amount of study and the additional year of internship that were required, and the difficult state medical examination in forensic medicine that had to be taken and passed in order to become board-certified. Dr. Eckert was a board-certified forensic pathologist; Dr. Vachal was not. And compared to her five hundred autopsies, his numbered over twelve thousand. Richard Hodson could feel his stomach slowly knotting.

The judge qualified Eckert as an expert witness, and a moment later Ricklin Pierce rushed into the courtroom and sat down in the empty chair next to Hodson. He was disappointed to have missed Eva Vachal's testimony, but he was delighted to find that Dr. Eckert had just been called to the stand. He sat quietly and watched, while Hodson listened and took notes.

Quint began by asking the doctor about when and where he had performed his re-autopsy of José Lumbrera and who had been in attendance that day. Then he got into specifics.

"Have you had an opportunity to review any of the previous autopsy documentation that was done by Dr. Vachal?"

"Dr. Vachal was nice enough to send me a copy

by fax that she had done at that time, which I was—I don't believe was the final [report], but it did provide the information that was important to me to find out what she had actually done," replied Eckert graciously.

"Have you further had an opportunity to see her final report?"

"No, I can't say, except—what I did see was the microscopic of that report, and that was today."

"Okay. The microscopic being the toxicology reports?" clarified Quint.

"Oh, no. Microscopic would be individual examination of each organ done in paraffin and stained, and then I—she sent—was nice enough, again, to send it to me so that I had occasion to review it. And then I sent back a note to you telling you of my findings."

". . . Have you had opportunity to visit with Dr. Vachal?"

"I have never met Dr. Vachal . . . except over the phone."

Then Quint focused on Eckert's examination of the body. "Your evaluation of José Lumbrera is based upon examination of what object or what subjects?" he asked.

"Well, his body."

"Okay. Did you have the benefit of his entire body?"

"There were parts of the body," explained the pathologist, ". . . the organs were—remained in the body, except the larynx was kept by Dr. Vachal, which I did not have occasion to see. She did describe it as not having anything major wrong with it, and she did send the slides, which included the larynx."

Pierce leaned forward, unable to believe his ears. Dr. Eckert had just testified that he had had *all* of the child's organs in his possession except the larynx. But Pierce knew that Eva Vachal had never sent many of those organs to Dr. Eckert, because he had never requested them from her. He looked over at Quint. The defense attorney had no outward reaction to the doctor's comment.

Pierce wondered if he had heard the doctor correctly. He looked at Hodson, but Hodson was acting as if nothing important had just happened. In fact, Hodson was completely unaware of the fact that Dr. Vachal had retained many of those organs. Pierce barely breathed while he listened to further testimony.

Quint asked the witness about the colored photographs that had been taken at the autopsy by the KBI agents and by the private detectives whom Quint had hired. Then he asked the doctor to explain his autopsy procedure, step by step, and to identify the photographs that documented each step so that they could be entered into evidence.

Dr. Eckert began with a photo of the child's closed coffin, then moved to a photo of the coffin as it lay open on the floor, exposing the clothed body of José Lumbrera. Another one showed the little teddy bear that had been tucked beneath the child's arm; still another showed the child's body without clothes. And soon others followed that revealed the graphic details of the dissection of the child's body.

The photographs and verbal descriptions were so disturbing that Quint interrupted Dr. Eckert to make a request of the court. He asked that anyone who might be feeling faint be allowed to leave the courtroom at that time. The judge agreed, and several people in the visitors' gallery quickly stood up and left.

Dr. Eckert continued to discuss his procedure while displaying the documenting photographs. It was a long, arduous, gory presentation, but Quint felt it necessary. He wanted the court to clearly understand how Dr. Eckert had reached his conclusion that the child had died from natural causes.

When the doctor neared the end of his presentation, he again mentioned seeing the child's organs.

"Seventy-five is a picture of the base of the skull with the top of the skull removed to demonstrate the presence of any injuries that may have occurred in the skull itself. In other words, any fractures or any bleeding that may have occurred. Number 76 . . . and 77 are pretty much the same. These show the organs that were placed in a bag and put in his body cavities, which enabled me to examine each individual organ of his chest, the brain, and the abdominal cavity. They were all there. The only thing that was missing, as I mentioned previously, was the larynx; and these are most—or these are all the pictures, I think."

Pierce could hardly believe their good fortune. Hodson had just been handed the ammunition he would need to destroy the famous doctor's entire testimony. Who would trust Eckert's findings after learning that he hadn't even seen some of those organs he was describing in such fascinating detail?

He looked at Quint again—no reaction. Then he looked at Hodson and saw that he wasn't reacting to Eckert's testimony either. He jotted the information on a scrap of paper and pushed it over in front of him.

Hodson ignored the note, his concentration fixed on Eckert's testimony. Pierce found it very difficult not to lean over and poke Hodson and share the exciting news with him right then. But he didn't.

When it was Hodson's turn to cross-examine Eckert, he tried to force the doctor to reveal which organ system or systems the viral infection had shut down in order to cause the death of José Lumbrera.

". . . the virus attacked the lungs; the lungs shut down; death resulted," offered Hodson in an attempt to clarify what he thought the doctor meant.

"Well, I think that's a generalization which cer— certainly can be applicable. I mean, it's— it's a— either is a focal infection involving one organ or the whole body, a diffuse process."

"Your diagnosis in this case is a diffuse process?"

"Yes, sir."

"Would that cause *all* of the organs to shut down?"

"Well, you know, when you say 'shut down,' you're talking physio— physiology, and a pathologist doesn't get into the physiology very much."

"Well, I understand that, doctor. I'm trying to

translate your medical opinion into laymen's terms that another attorney and a judge can understand."

"Certainly."

One of the problems trial lawyers often have in cases like these is not knowing the right questions to ask. That kind of ignorance can enable a medical expert to hide behind complicated medical terms and extraneous possibilities and confuse the issues, with no one becoming the wiser. That was just what was happening here. Hodson tried hard to make some sense out of what the doctor was saying, but the man refused to be pinned down. Eckert finally said that one possibility was that the child had died from toxins that had been produced by the virus.

"What kind of cause of death, then, in a situation like that?" Hodson asked with growing frustration in his voice.

"Toxic— toxemia is a basic cause, which is due— produced by the infective process. The— when a— when a bug such as a bacteria and a viru— and there were— virus gets in the body, they may produce toxins which themselves— they— which in itself— in themselves could cause a major problem and death."

"What— in a situation of toxemia or other production of toxins—"

"Yes, sir?" said the skilled witness, smiling.

". . . what evidence would you find of that after death or in the autopsy?"

"If— if a serology was drawn on this child at the time of the autopsy and done postmortem, there may well have been identified some toxic product which could be examined for a specific agent, such— either virus or bacteria."

"Doctor, I would— I'm sorry. You are dealing with— with lay people. What is a serology?"

After another half hour of frustration, Hodson gave up and returned to his chair. Then Eckert was excused and the hearing adjourned for the day.

The minute the judge left the courtroom, the press swarmed into action. Quint had not let Diana return, so there were no more chances to take photos of her. The eager reporters and their camera crews gathered around Diana's younger sister, Isabel, who had just walked out into the hallway.

Isabel had two small children at home and was seven months pregnant with her third. And she was certain that Diana had not murdered her own children. With hostility in her voice she told the reporters how stupid it was to think that Diana had killed her only surviving child.

". . . that girl has just worked so hard to try to support that kid and herself," she said.

Inside the courtroom Pierce was telling Hodson of Dr. Eckert's amazing blunder. The two men discussed whether they should bring back Dr. Vachal for rebuttal and completely discredit Eckert or wait until the trial. They decided to wait. The case would probably go to trial, and Pierce would need something this incredible if he hoped to get a conviction.

The preliminary hearing lasted two more days. Hodson brought in evidence of Diana's serious financial condition, evidence of her five other dead children, and evidence of incriminating statements she had made during her interviews with the police. By the time the prelim ended, Hodson had called a total of fourteen witnesses, and he had recalled four of them to testify a second time. He guessed that it was overkill, but he wanted to be sure.

Judge Heath's decision came late on the afternoon of Friday, June 15, 1990, after the last witness had stepped down. Unlike juries, Judge Heath was not easily dazzled by bigger-than-life reputations. He was a practical individual who judged things on the basis of whether or not they made sense to him. And Dr. Vachal's clear, precise explanations had made better sense to him than the vague explanations offered by Dr. Eckert. He had decided to bind Diana Lumbrera over for formal arraignment and trial.

The judge announced his decision and told the deputy to take the defendant back into custody. Then he pounded his gavel and brought the prelim to an official close.

Diana stared up at the judge in disbelief as his words slowly sank in. She couldn't believe this was happening to her, and she became frightened. She grabbed Quint by the coat sleeve and pleaded with him to tell her why. She didn't even notice the flock of cameramen who had moved to the front of the courtroom to get a close-up of her face.

The judge's decision had also surprised Quint. He reassured his client and silently guessed that the judge's knowledge of Diana's other dead children had affected his decision. He had to find a way to keep that information out of the trial or Diana wouldn't stand a chance.

Chapter 23

The Texas investigation was nearly finished when Deputy Jerry Bailey and Detective James Hawkins made yet another startling discovery. Bailey had driven up to Garden City to interview Diana about the Texas deaths, but she had refused to talk to him, so he had gone with Hawkins to interview a witness. The two men drove to a modest neighborhood in a small town north of Garden City where Diana's first husband lived. The man's name was Mario Jaramillo, and he was living with his current wife and two small children.

The house was small, clean, and neatly furnished. A vase of red and pink roses decorated the old wooden dining table around which Jaramillo and the two lawmen sat. Jaramillo was on his lunch hour, so he ate hot cheese enchiladas as he talked.

Jaramillo said that a few months after he and Diana had split up, she called him from New Mexico and told him that she had given birth to his baby, a little girl she had called Jessica. She said the child had suddenly died and that a funeral was about to be held, but that he would not be allowed to attend.

Jaramillo said that before their separation she had never mentioned that she was pregnant, so he had not known whether or not she was telling him the truth. He still didn't know, because she had lied so often about other things.

Bailey took that information back to Texas, then contacted Jim Dickins, chief investigator of the Ninth Judicial District in Clovis, New Mexico. A check of the county records in New Mexico and Texas failed to turn up any documentation on an infant named Jessica Jaramillo or Jessica Lumbrera.

However, Bailey knew that there was a lot of vacant land in that corner of New Mexico, and it would have been very easy to bury a small body unseen without the expense of a regular funeral. After all, Diana would have been sixteen years old at the time and without insurance, and her family was also very poor. But whether Jessica had ever lived and died, or whether she was the first of eight victims would remain a moot question. Without documentation or a witness who would talk, no one would ever know for sure.

If the investigators found Diana's tale of a possible eighth victim interesting, the media found it fascinating. It gave them a startling headline to use after the news of her preliminary hearing had become old business. The tone of the news stories about Diana suddenly changed, and they no longer portrayed her as the innocent victim of a "trigger happy prosecutor." Instead they focused on the drama surrounding the unfolding of the case and of her impending trial.

As the days slipped by, the remaining leads were followed up while the investigators in both states waited anxiously for the opinions of Dr. Baden in New York, Dr. Bux in Texas, and a third pathologist in Colorado named Dr. Harry Wilson.

The Kempe National Center had recommended Dr. Wilson because he was a pediatric pathologist at Children's Hospital in Denver and was an excellent "microscope" man. In other words, Wilson would be able to determine whether or not José Lumbrera had died of a viral infection, and if he had not, Wilson's testimony would refute that of Dr. Eckert. Wilson wasn't a "big name" in his profession, but he was highly respected for both his skills and his dedication to saving children's lives. Hawkins had called him and like Baden, Wilson had immediately agreed to help.

Pierce was feeling an increasing sense of urgency about getting back the pathologists' results. He knew the Texas district attorneys would need those results in order to obtain murder indictments against Diana. He would need those Texas indictments if he hoped to convince a judge to allow him to mention the six Texas murders at Diana's trial in Kansas. And he would need to mention those murders at the trial if he hoped to convince a jury that José was simply the last of Diana's seven victims.

The events were as dependent on each other as a line of falling dominoes, and the hearing to determine the admissibility of those Texas murders in the Kansas trial was scheduled for August 15. There wasn't a lot of time left.

Diana's formal arraignment was held in early July, and no one was surprised when she entered a plea of not guilty. The surprise came when a friend of the Lumbrera family drove up from Texas and posted Diana's $50,000 bond. Diana had been a prisoner in the Finney County Jail for over three months, and many things had changed during that time.

The insurance company had refused to pay off the child's life insurance policy unless Diana was found not-guilty at her murder trial. And with no other source of income, she had been forced to give up her small duplex apartment. Once out of jail, she moved in with her younger sister, Isabel, and her family in Garden City. Isabel wasn't worried about Diana being around her children because, like the rest of the Lumbrera family, she clung to the belief that Diana was innocent. Diana hung around the house for a few days, then went back to work at the Monfort plant.

Pierce and the detectives had been waiting nervously to see if Diana would flee their jurisdiction, and they couldn't help but wonder why she had chosen to stay. They finally concluded that since she had always been able to lie her way out of trouble, she thought she could do it again. She would play the part of a grieving mother and the jury would believe her. It was that simple.

By the end of July, Drs. Baden, Bux, and Wilson had completed their analyses and submitted their reports. Based on the medical history of the children, Diana's medical history, the circumstances surrounding each of the deaths, the findings of the autopsies, and an examination of all available tissue slides and autopsy photographs, the pathologists agreed that the children had all died from asphyxia due to suffocation, probably from smothering.

The doctors also agreed on one other thing: Diana would *always* be a danger to any child left in her care.

As soon as Johnny Actkinson learned of their findings, he scheduled a meeting of the Parmer County grand jury for August 7. It was during the preparation for that meeting that Actkinson finally became convinced of Diana's guilt.

He and his assistant, Luther Thompson, had organized the information that had been collected on the six Texas deaths into a detailed matrix. When it was finished, Diana's killing pattern emerged clearly. Actkinson was startled when he saw how obvious it actually was.

That afternoon, the twelve members of the grand jury began arriving at the old courthouse in Farwell. They parked their cars and pickup trucks in the dirt parking lot by the side of the building, then headed for the jury room. They all gathered around the long, rectangular wooden table, which was positioned in the center of the room beneath a bank of hot fluorescent lights. A portable fan in the corner turned slowly back and forth, circulating the warm air and making the room barely tolerable.

The hearing was not only a criminal proceeding but a media event, so the corridor outside the room was filled with reporters and their camera crews. They stood waiting restlessly for a chance to get something for the five o'clock news and the late-edition newspapers. Everyone wanted to know if Texas was going to pursue its prosecution of Diana Lumbrera.

Standing together at the end of the corridor were Actkinson's only witnesses—Deputies Bailey and Bonham and Texas Ranger Warren Yeager. Although Actkinson was going to show the "whole picture" to the grand jury, it had jurisdiction over only the three deaths that had occurred in Parmer County. Those deaths included that of three-month-old Joanna, the first victim; three-year-old Melissa, the third victim; and two-year-old Melinda, the fifth victim.

Nearly three hours had passed before Actkinson finished presenting the evidence on the sixth and last Texas death, that of five-month-old Christopher. When Actkinson left the room for the grand jury to deliberate, the press rushed over. He explained that it might take some time before a decision was reached and asked them to be patient. In fact, only two minutes passed before the jury foreman poked his head outside the door and asked Actkinson to come back in. They had indicted Diana on three counts of capital murder, a crime punishable by a life sentence or the death penalty if she was found guilty.

In Garden City, it was Elliott's day off, so Hawkins and Utz quickly made arrangements for Diana's arrest on the Texas warrants. They contacted a uniformed patrol officer named Jack Belland and told him to meet them at the address where Diana was staying.

The sister's house was very small, with a tiny front lawn enclosed by a split-rail fence. Diana's car was parked in the driveway. All three men walked to the door, and the sister opened it.

Isabel recognized the detectives and immediately became apprehensive; she didn't know why they were there, but she knew it meant trouble. She let them enter, then called to Diana, who was in a room at the rear of the small house. When Diana came into the living room and saw the detectives, she stopped dead and stared. It was Hawkins who spoke first.

"Diana, we have a warrant for your arrest from Texas, and we'd like you to come with us now."

Diana couldn't believe what she was hearing. She knew that some kind of investigation had been going on in Texas; she had read that much in the newspapers. But she had never thought for an instant that they'd find anything.

Her first reaction was exasperation, but it quickly turned into rage. Officer Belland stepped behind her, grabbed her wrists and handcuffed her.

Diana's sister demanded to know why Diana was

continually being harassed. She screamed that such treatment wasn't fair, because Diana was innocent. A small, frightened child toddled into the living room and began to cry.

Diana demanded to call her attorney, so Hawkins told her that she could call him from jail. He didn't bother to Mirandize her, because he had no intention of asking her any questions. Belland led her outside, put her in the back of the patrol car, and headed for the LEC. No bond would be set on the Texas charges.

Chapter 24

When the Associated Press sent word of the Kansas and Texas indictments through the country's newspapers, calls began to come in from interested newsmagazines and talk shows. A producer from CBS's *60 Minutes* and producers from two other network talk shows called to get details of the case. Joe Don Buckner, photography manager for the *Lubbock Avalanche Journal*, sold copyrighted photos of Diana to newspapers all over the nation, plus three newspapers in England and one in Norway. People wanted to know about this woman who killed children for fun and money.

But no one connected with the investigation in either state would talk to the media—not the prosecutors, not the investigators, not even the medical personnel. It was far too risky. Everyone agreed that any discussion would have to wait until Diana was convicted and no chance remained that she would go free.

As for Pierce, he had more important things to

think about. Diana's scheduled hearing was only a week away, and the outcome of that hearing would determine whether or not he would be allowed to introduce evidence of the Texas murders into the Kansas trial. He knew he would need the help of the Texas lawmen in order to develop a convincing argument, so he arranged for them to travel to Garden City the day before the hearing.

The three men drove up together and arrived at Pierce's office shortly after lunch. The news of their impending arrival had leaked to the media, and they descended on the lawmen as soon as they walked through the door. The three large Texans were an impressive sight. Bailey and Bonham wore dark business suits and cowboy boots. Yeager wore a white shirt and tie, dress Levi's, and a white Stetson. A .45 automatic was holstered on his hip.

Once the press left, Pierce walked the men over to the LEC to meet their counterparts. Bailey had met everyone but Pierce during his trip to Garden City, but it was Yeager's and Bonham's first face-to-face meeting with the Kansas detectives. Soon hands were being shaken, backs slapped, and jokes exchanged as the men greeted one another.

This was also the first time any of the Kansas people had met a Texas Ranger, and Yeager, with his handsome cowboy image, didn't disappoint them. When the word went out that the Texas Ranger was in the building, people gathered in the hallways hoping to catch a glimpse of him.

Fifteen minutes later, Pierce and the Texans were seated around the long rectangular table in the departmental library, where they could work without distraction. Pierce didn't have a copy of the matrix Johnny Actkinson had created the week before, so they started from scratch and worked together, creating one after another until Pierce finally had what he needed. Then he looked up, smiled and said, "This is it. No one in the world could look at this and not be convinced that Diana had murdered all seven of those children."

Pierce's enthusiasm was tempered by fear that the judge would find the information in the matrix too prejudicial to be admitted into trial. That is, the judge might decide that it would create such strong prejudice in the minds of the jurors that they would be convinced of Diana's guilt even if presented with sufficient evidence of her innocence. Pierce figured he had about one shot in three of getting the judge to let it in, and he thought it only fair to share his concerns with the three lawmen.

"You know, we shouldn't get our hopes up. But, on the other hand," he added, "if we win this hearing, we've won this case. This is basically the trial right here. If the judge allows this stuff, we've got it made, and it's all over after today."

"You're right," Yeager agreed, as he leaned back in his chair and stretched. "No jury is gonna acquit her after they see something like this."

The work was over, so only the waiting was left. They would know the judge's decision before twenty-four hours had passed.

The following afternoon, when Judge Stephen Nyswonger entered the courtroom, Pierce, Quint, and Diana Lumbrera were already waiting quietly at their counsel tables. A court reporter sat ready at her machine. Outside in the hallway were gathered Pierce's witnesses: Bailey, Bonham, Yeager, Elliott, and Hawkins.

Diana was dressed in a soft red blouse and a pair of Levi's that had once been skintight; now they hung loosely. On her feet were a pair of plain black pumps. She had washed her hair the night before, so it was full, clean, and shiny. But she had awakened in an irritable mood and hadn't bothered to put on any makeup. Her bad mood was obvious, and when Pierce stood up to begin his presentation, she looked over and glowered at him.

Pierce walked between the defense table and the judge's bench, where he had positioned two large white marker boards on rollers. He had already created the outlines of his matrix using a black marker pen. He nervously called his first witness, Deputy Bonham, to the stand.

Pierce had Bonham verbally list the names of Diana's five children who had died in Texas and the name of her cousin's infant, Ericka Aleman. As the deputy gave each name, Pierce printed it in large red letters along the top of the matrix. When he was finished, there were three names at the top of each board.

Pierce next wrote his first characteristic at the top of the columns along the left margins: "age at time of death." He had the deputy tell him at what age each child had suddenly died, and then he marked that age into each child's respective column.

Pierce wrote his next characteristic on the two boards. It was "cause of death."

"Pursuant to your investigation of these four deaths did you make any contact with forensic pathologists?"

"Yes, I did."

Bonham described how he had sent Dr. Robert Bux copies of the children's autopsies and the microscopic slides of tissues that had been taken during those autopsies.

"Now, have you had an opportunity talk with Dr. Bux after he completed all of his work on these matters?"

"Yes, I have."

"How long ago was that telephone call?"

"Approximately a week and a half ago."

"And what did he say in regard to his examination and study?"

In a trial such second-party information would have been inadmissible as "hearsay," but not in a hearing of this type. Bonham answered the question.

". . . he stated he was just about completed [with] his investigation into our autopsies and autopsy slides. At that time he revealed to me that . . . he was ruling [them] as homicide, either by smothering or by suffocation."

In each child's column Pierce wrote the determined cause of death, "smothering/suffocation."

Both boards sat less than six feet to the left of Diana's face, and the names of her dead children and the causes of their deaths showed up brightly against the white background. But her face showed no expression as she gazed out the large windows on the opposite side of the courtroom.

Pierce then instructed Bonham to give answers about only the four deaths he had personally investigated as they went through the rest of the characteristics. Soon the list along the left margin included age at time of death; insurance amount, beneficiary, and source; hospital where Diana had taken her dying or dead child; whether or not an autopsy had been performed; listed cause of death; any delay in seeking treatment; person(s) with child when it stopped breathing; treating physician; person giving treating physician possible diagnosis; and whether or not the child had been receiving medical attention in the days preceding its death.

When Bonham had finished giving all the information that pertained to the four deaths he had investigated, Pierce asked his next question.

"How many of those cases are in Parmer County?"

"Three."

"And the other one, what county was that in?"

"Ericka Aleman's case is in Bailey County, which is the same judicial district for the district attorney's office in the 287th District Court."

"Now, sir, in Parmer County has a grand jury been convened in regard to the deaths in Parmer County?"

"Yes, they have."

"And did they come back with an indictment?"

"Yes."

"How many?"

"Three indictments for capital murder."

"And what's the penalty for capital murder?"

"Life imprisonment or death."

"Your Honor, I have no further questions for this witness."

If the threat of one or more possible impending death sentences frightened Diana, no one could tell. She continued to remain immobile and emotionless as she stared blindly out the window.

Pierce next called Warren Yeager to the stand.

Yeager was sworn in, then he testified to the facts surrounding the death of José Luís Garza, Diana's two-mouth-old son who had died while in Methodist Hospital. His column was the fifth to be filled, and the similarities of all five deaths were blatantly obvious. It was hard for the judge not to be overwhelmed by what he saw.

Pierce called up Deputy Jerry Bailey to finish the Texas deaths. Bailey gave the matrix information for five-month-old Christopher, who had died in Castro County, Bailey's jurisdiction. Bailey was also allowed to tell about the efforts Dr. Kyle Mason had made in his attempt to save Christopher from the same fate his siblings had met.

Pierce's next witness was Detective Ken Elliott. Elliott talked about the details surrounding the death of four-year-old José Antonio Lumbrera in Garden City.

And finally Pierce called Detective James Hawkins and had him explain about the findings of Drs. Baden and Wilson.

Diana's killing pattern stood out starkly on the two boards: Each of the seven victims had been under five years of age; all had been alone with Diana at the time they died; in each incident, Diana had delayed seeking treatment when the child stopped breathing; all had been previously hospitalized, and Diana had offered her own diagnoses to the doctors during those hospitalizations; each child had had life insurance, and Diana had been the beneficiary. Only one child showed any variance from this pattern—Ericka Aleman, the infant daughter of her cousins. This child had not been previously sick, and Diana had not profited financially from its death. All other factors were the same.

And there were the expert medical opinions of Drs. Baden, Bux, and Wilson regarding the cause of the children's deaths. These experts all agreed that the children's deaths had not been natural but had probably been the result of smothering.

From where Pierce was standing, he could clearly see Mike Quint and Diana Lumbrera, and he had periodically glanced at them while the investigators had given their evidence. Diana had looked at only two of the witnesses, Hawkins and Elliott, and both times her eyes had been filled with cold, raw hatred.

Pierce had also seen Quint carefully studying the matrix. But if the information of the matrix had convinced Quint of Diana's guilt, he made sure no one could tell. The skilled defense attorney kept his features set firmly in place.

When all evidence had been presented, the judge

called a recess while he made up his mind. Thirty minutes later he called the session back to order to give his ruling.

"For the record, I've had an opportunity to try to reflect upon the evidence that I've heard for the last day concerning the State's request to introduce evidence of prior crimes . . . and the defendant's motion . . . and case authority under Kansas law."

Then the judge cited various case precedents and how they applied to the matter at hand. One by one he eliminated the six possible rules under which the previous deaths might have been allowed in at the trial. And with each ruling Pierce's gut tied into a tighter and tighter knot.

Finally the judge came to the bottom line of his decision.

"I rule and find that the prejudice outweighs the probative value, and the State's request . . . is denied."

Pierce felt like a fist had just knocked all the air out of him. He turned and saw Diana staring at him, a look of smugness on her face.

Oh, no, he thought angrily, returning her stare, it may take a fight, but you're not getting away with murder this time.

PART IV

THE TRIAL

Chapter 25

A determined, overly plump woman in a dark blue suit pushed her way toward the only remaining seat in the visitors' gallery. She squeezed into the small space, ignored the discomfort her presence caused the two older men sitting next to her, and looked curiously around the courtroom.

The room was large and decorated in somber tones of gray and brown—stucco wall panels, oak furniture, neutral carpeting, a high acoustical ceiling. A bank of overhead fluorescent lights brightened the room, and tall windows along one side gave it the illusion of being even larger.

The woman sighed with disappointment at the obvious renovation. Years ago she had read Truman Capote's famous book *In Cold Blood,* and she knew that the killers of the Clutter family had been tried in this very room. She had hoped that the room would still be in its original condition.

The door behind the judge's bench suddenly swung open and a deputy sheriff walked in. Necks craned as Diana followed behind him, her attorney at her side. Diana looked thin and attractive in a dark pantsuit. Someone in the row behind the plump woman whispered, "She doesn't look like a baby killer, does she?" Then everyone watched as Diana glanced innocently at the crowd, pulled out a chair at the defense table, and sat down beside Mike Quint.

Quint removed a stack of papers from his briefcase and laid them on the table. Next he removed a box of Kleenex and a large family Bible and placed them in front of Diana. His biggest concern was how Diana would appear to the jury. During her earlier court hearings she had sat passively, devoid of any expression during the discussions of her dead children. Quint knew that a judge might be able to ignore such behavior, but a jury would not. He hoped these stage props would remind Diana to let her emotions show and would help the jury to see her as a grieving mother of deep religious faith.

The door swung open again, and Ricklin Pierce and his new assistant county attorney, Mary Ann Shirley, walked into the room. They took their places at the other counsel table, then Shirley quickly laid out their papers and notebooks and organized the prepared exhibits.

In her early forties, Shirley had curly reddish-brown hair, soft features, and a fair share of common sense. Her job would be to take notes of the witnesses' statements and to stay alert for any unusual reactions made by the witnesses or jury.

While his colleague organized their materials,

Pierce quickly reviewed his notes. He had prepared well for this trial, including working with Dr. Vachal to learn the medical terms and processes that related to the child's death. Dr. Eckert wouldn't be able to confuse the issues this time. Only one thing was worrying him: Would Dr. Eckert repeat the same mistake about the missing organs? If he didn't, Pierce knew his case would be in trouble.

Not being allowed to mention Diana's other dead children was no longer as important. The press reports had been mentioning those deaths and their similarities daily, and almost everyone living within a hundred-mile radius now knew about them—including many of the jurors.

By nine o'clock the back wall was lined with reporters and curious spectators, people who were willing to stand just to see the unfolding drama of the Lumbrera trial.

A few minutes later Judge Stephen Nyswonger entered the courtroom wearing his long black robe. Pierce felt a sudden surge of adrenaline as the bailiff told everyone present to rise. Then thirteen jurors walked in single file and took their seats in the jury box. One juror had already called in sick.

Pierce was satisfied with the jury that had been selected; Quint was not. The prosecutor's strategy of jury selection had been simple. He was willing to accept anyone who wasn't biased, who hadn't lost a child of any age, and who hadn't suffered a recent, painful loss of a family member. He didn't want anyone sitting on the jury who would identify with the grief Quint would be trying to say Diana was feeling. And Pierce thought he had managed to eliminate everyone who did not fit that profile, so he felt hopeful that the jury would be fair.

Quint's strategy had been predictably different. He was looking for individuals who could understand how a child could suddenly become ill and die—like parents of young children. But he also wanted individuals who were knowledgeable about the Hispanic culture and who could understand how a belief in the powers of the evil *brujos* might affect a Hispanic mother's behavior.

Jury selection had taken two entire days, and when it was over more than 130 individuals had been questioned and released. The fourteen people finally selected were equally divided by sex, mostly middle-aged, and all Caucasian, except for one Hispanic woman. Once the jury was sworn in, both attorneys gave their opening statements, then Pierce began the presentation of his case.

As Hodson did at the prelim, Pierce first called the medical staff of St. Catherine's emergency room to prove that José had not been sick enough to die from natural causes. Then Dr. Vachal took the stand and explained her autopsy results; the child had died from smothering.

Once again Diana listened without expression. If she was trying to play the grieving mother, it wasn't working because she obviously wasn't excited; she was bored. After an initial attempt at crying, she soon gave up and stared out the windows instead. She never bothered to use the tissues or open the Bible.

By late afternoon the courtroom had become unbearably warm. The ceiling was too high for the weak air-conditioning system, and there were no ceiling fans to suck up the hot air. Even those who were dressed in cotton clothing were fanning themselves in a futile attempt to cool off.

Judge Nyswonger looked at this watch, wiped the sweat from his brow, and called a recess for the day.

Over the next few days Pierce called his remaining witnesses and had them add to the story of a mother who had killed her son for money. One of his best witnesses was Joan Steadwell, the loan officer from Diana's credit union. Joan described Diana's spiraling descent into serious debt and the false stories Diana had told her about José's fatal disease. Diana's supervisor at Monfort said that Diana had told her similar stories. Pierce hoped the jury would see how Diana had used those stories to manipulate those individuals and to prepare them for José's inevitable sudden death.

Then came the detectives who testified about the stack of overdue bills, the vials of unused medicine, and the pitiful collection of José's toys they had found while searching Diana's apartment. They also told of the incriminating statements she had made.

On the fourth day Pierce called Christina Hernandez, José's godmother, to the stand. When Mrs. Hernandez walked into the room the whispering stopped and people stared. Her face was swollen to the size of a large balloon from recent surgery on her left ear. Pierce winced as he looked at her, then reminded himself that he had no choice; this had to be done.

Pierce had called her to testify so that he could introduce one of the photographs of José he had found in Diana's apartment. His reason was simple. For three days the jury had heard the child's name repeated over and over. They had heard discussed the circumstances of his death, the condition of his dead body, the facts of his funeral. They had seen the photos of the home in which he had lived and the photos of the beds on which he had slept. They had even seen and felt the sheets on which he had died.

But so far José Antonio Lumbrera was just the name of a dead child—an abstract concept in their minds. Pierce wanted the jurors to see what José had looked like when he was alive. He wanted them to see the happy little boy who had trusted his mother.

"Was Diana Lumbrera living with you when José Lumbrera was born?" he asked.

"Yes."

". . . After the child was born, did you become the godmother of the child?"

"Yes."

"And did you see the child frequently from that point to today?"

"Yes."

". . . how would you describe José Lumbrera?"

"A child that loved to play." Her voice began to choke as tears came to her eyes.

"Was he active?"

"Yes, he was."

"Now, do you recall the evening before he died?"

"Yes."

"Was José Lumbrera at your house, let's say in the early morning hours of May the 1st?"

"On the 1st."

"May 1st?"

"Yes, he was."

"Why was he at your house at that time?"

"She took him to the hospital," said Mrs. Hernandez, looking at Diana as she spoke, "and from the hospital she took him to my home."

"And was 'she' Diana Lumbrera?"

"Yes," she said, lowering her eyes.

"Do you recall at what time José and Diana Lumbrera came to your house?"

"About 11 o'clock at night."

"And that would have been the evening prior to his death; is that correct?"

"Yes."

"When did José Lumbrera and Diana Lumbrera leave your house?"

"About 1:30 in the morning of the following day."

"And that would have been the day that he died; is that correct?"

"Yes, sir."

"Now, did José Lumbrera throw up or get sick when he was in your house from 11 o'clock on April 30th to one o'clock on May the 1st?"

"No, he did not throw up."

"What did he do when he was at your house?"

"He was asleep from the time he arrived to the time he left."

"Did he leave with Diana Lumbrera then?"

"Yes."

"Now, after he left, did you ever see José Lumbrera after that alive?"

"At 4:30 in the evening I did."

That last question brought back images that had been seared into the woman's memory, and it became harder for her to talk.

"And that would have been the evening that he had died; is that correct?" Pierce asked.

"Yes, sir."

"Where were you when you saw him at 4:30 in the afternoon?"

"At the stop light . . . at the corner of 4th and Fulton."

"Were you in an automobile at the time?"

"Yes, sir."

". . . did you see José Lumbrera in another vehicle at that time?"

"Yes."

"And who was José with at the time?"

Tears were streaming down Mrs. Hernandez's face, so the judge stopped the questions for a moment and handed her a box of Kleenex. She wiped at the tears, then took a moment to compose herself. Finally she continued.

"Yes, with his mother."

"Thank you," Pierce said compassionately. "Was there anyone else in the car besides his mother and José?"

"I didn't see anyone."

"Can you give us a brief description of the car they were in?"

"It was a white car of hers," she said, motioning toward Diana.

"Did José do anything at this time when you were at that stoplight?"

"Just waved at me."

"He recognized you; is that correct?"

"Yes."

"And what did you do?"

"I answered him back."

"And how?"

"The same way." Then, as she slowly waved her right hand to show how she had waved back at him, her tears suddenly gave way to deep, heartfelt sobs.

No one in the courtroom moved; it would have felt sacrilegious to make a sound in the midst of such genuine human suffering. Few even breathed as long seconds ticked by. There was no doubt in anyone's mind that this woman's grief was very deep and very painful.

Mary Ann glanced at Diana Lumbrera to catch her reaction. She seemed completely detached from everything around her as she stared blankly down at the table. Then Mary Ann noticed that some of the jurors were also looking at Diana. She wondered what they saw: a grieving mother still in shock from the sudden loss of her only child or a cold-blooded killer without feelings?

Pierce felt uncomfortable continuing, but he had no choice.

"Now, Mrs. Hernandez, I'm going to show you

State's Exhibit 51 and ask if you can identify that person?" Pierce held up José's photograph.

"Yes, I know."

"Who is it?"

"José Antonio Lumbrera," she sobbed.

The photograph was entered into evidence, then Pierce released the witness, handed the photograph to one of the jurors to be passed around, and returned to his chair.

After the last witness of the day had testified, Pierce and Shirley lugged the large stacks of files and notebooks upstairs to his office. It was sheer chance that they walked in the office door before the switchboard closed for the day, or that Pierce was even there to take a telephone call. But just at that moment a man named Chester Williams telephoned and asked to speak to the prosecuting attorney. Williams was the landlord of the duplex where Diana had been living when José died. He had one question he wanted Pierce to answer: Was it true that little José had not died of leukemia?

Pierce had originally asked the detectives to interview Williams to obtain information on the amount of rent Diana had paid and how often those payments were late. It was information that Pierce needed in order to compile an accurate record of Diana's monthly expenses and accrued debt.

The detectives obtained that information, but Williams did not offer them anything more at the time. He revealed as little as possible, because he was another believer in Diana's innocence, and he didn't want to help in what he thought was an unjust prosecution. But now he was beginning to have his doubts, and he needed an answer to his question.

Pierce assured him that the autopsy of the child, which had been performed by Dr. Vachal and later confirmed by two other highly qualified pathologists, had shown that the only thing wrong with the child had been a very small cold. The child had not died a natural death; he had been smothered. Williams was quiet for a moment, then he offered Pierce the information he had been keeping to himself. Pierce arranged to have him testify early the following day.

The spectators watched as Chester Williams walked into the courtroom and up to the witness stand. He was a short man of about fifty years of age with a dark flap of hair worn over a balding head. Dressed in clean jeans and a work shirt, he was a good-hearted man who took no joy in what he was about to do.

Pierce began by asking him about Diana's rent payments, and he explained that Diana had paid $275 monthly for her duplex apartment, plus approximately $75 for utilities. She had been late a number of times, but he had always trusted her to eventually make up those payments, and she always had done so.

"Now, did you have a custom or habit of going to the apartment to collect that rent?" Pierce asked.

"With Diana, sometimes she would come by my house and pay rent. If I was over there I would collect the rent while I was there. . . ."

"Now, I'm going to refer your attention to Tuesday, May 1, 1990. Did you go over to that address on Tonio Street to collect rent from Diana Lumbrera?"

"Yes, I did. I'd been out of town over that previous weekend, and I thought maybe she'd been by the house. So, I stopped by there that evening to see if she was home." Williams glanced at Diana, but she kept her eyes downward.

"And was anybody with you when you stopped by, sir?"

"My wife was with me."

"Were you both in an automobile at that time?"

"Yes."

"Did your wife go to the door with you?"

"No. She stayed in the car."

"Now, when you went to the door, do you recall approximately what time you arrived at that Tonio address?"

"Was somewhere between 7:00 and 7:30 P.M. I'd say probably closer to 7:00 than 7:30, but in that 30-minute period somewhere."

"And did you knock or ring a bell to find out if anyone was home?"

"I knocked on the door."

"And did anybody respond?"

"Diana answered the door."

"And could you see Diana when she answered the door?"

"Yes, I could."

"What sort of a screen is there on that particular apartment?"

"Well, there's a screen door, and it's a double screen, so it makes it hard to see in from the outside. You can see out from the inside, but it's— it's a little harder to see in from the outside."

"And was it dark at this time, sir?"

"Yes. Uh-huh."

"And did she pay you any money for the rent?"

"Not at that time, no. She told me that she would pay her rent Friday, which was pretty ordinary. I think she got paid either Thursday night or Friday morning, so she would generally pay it on Friday."

"And did you also give her a utility bill or just want to collect the rent at that time?"

"I think at that time I was just collecting the rent. I didn't have anything with me on utilities, no."

"Now, sir, did you recognize Diana Lumbrera's voice through the screen door?"

"Yes. I could see her."

"Was there anybody else in that apartment that you could either recognize or hear or possibly see?"

"I couldn't see anybody else. José was there. I could— could hear him. Anytime I was there he was always out to see me, and lots of times he'd stay around when we were there to do some work or something. He was always there."

"And he knew you; is that correct?"

"Oh, yeah."

"How could you tell José was there, sir?"

"He came to the door and wanted to come out to see me, and she told him to— to get back from the door, and he did. And I never did actually see him, but he was there. I could tell. Heard him."

"And she did address some other person that you could hear, and say, 'Get away from the door' or 'Get back from the door'?"

"Yes. Uh-huh."

Diana had told the detectives that José was deathly sick with a high fever that evening and that she had put him to bed at seven o'clock. Would a dying child be struggling to get out the door to see his friend, the landlord?

Pierce also wanted to know what Diana had told Chester Williams about José's medical condition. "Now, sir," he continued, "do you recall a particular incident when she came over to your house and talked about a medical condition of her son's?"

"Yes. One evening she came and paid part of the rent and said that she couldn't pay all of the rent, because she'd bought some high-priced medicine to treat her son's leukemia."

Half an hour later, Pierce rested his case, so the judge adjourned the trial for the day and announced that it would resume on Monday, October 1, after a three-day recess. At that time it would be Mike Quint's turn to present evidence for the defense.

Quint looked and sounded confident as he rose to his feet and called his defense witnesses to the stand one by one. These people were Diana's friends, coworkers, and acquaintances, people who believed that she had been a good mother to her child, that she had worked extra hours just to buy him special things, and that she had been deeply affected by his death. A friend of the child's baby-sitter remembered how ill José had been on the day he had died.

It was nearly two o'clock in the afternoon when Mike Quint turned toward the rear of the courtroom and called his star witness, Dr. William G. Eckert, to the stand.

In the weeks preceding the trial, Dr. Eva Vachal had made a careful study of Dr. Eckert's written works, and she had reached an interesting conclusion. In her opinion Eckert was a "trauma man," someone with considerable skill in the detection and analysis of traumatic wounds caused by weapons such as guns, knives, clubs, and poisons. She guessed that since no obvious marks had been left on José's dead body, except the petechiae on his face and neck and the linear hemorrhage in his right eye, Eckert had assumed that he couldn't have been smothered.

The famous pathologist strode confidently to the witness stand, the picture of self-assurance. He climbed onto the raised platform, turned toward the court clerk, and raised his right hand to be sworn in.

Diana was quickly escorted out of the courtroom, then Pierce watched intently as Quint asked the doctor to describe each stage of the autopsy he had performed on the child's body.

Quint couldn't use the same graphic photographs of the autopsy that he had used at Diana's preliminary hearing, because of the negative effect that such pictures would have on the jury. So he had created two other types of visual aids. One was enlarged photographs of the tissue samples, which

Eckert would use to discuss his microscopic findings. The other was an anatomical diagram of a human body, which he had placed on an easel near the doctor's chair. The doctor would use that chart to show the jury which area of the body he was referring to as he talked.

Eckert began by describing how he and the others present had removed the child's body from the small coffin. And how he had then removed the clothing, washed the body, and conducted an external examination. He described how he had looked for any evidence of previous injury.

"Was there anything in particular unusual from the gross examination of the exterior of the body?" asked Quint.

The doctor explained that only a few bruises were found on the child's right leg.

"Now, once you opened the body up again, was there any gross findings or any findings of any regard regarding the body cavity itself, for instance?" Quint asked.

Eckert removed a silver telescoping pointer from his jacket pocket, extended it to full length, then leaned forward and pointed toward the chart as he talked.

Eckert said there had been no fractures of the ribs or vertebrae, then added, "We could see organs that had been removed. They were still in the bag, and I examined those individually."

Pierce struggled to keep from smiling as he and Mary Ann Shirley exchanged a quick, surreptitious glance.

Quint did not know about Eckert's error at the prelim, or that his star witness had just made that same error again. He asked Eckert about his examination of each of those organs.

"In a gross examination of the heart did you see anything unusual?"

"No, sir. There was no evidence of any congenital anomalies or something that happened . . . during the early life of the child, and there was no evidence of any changes in the lungs, which are consistent with a congenital anomaly of the lung."

Quint asked about the arteries, the endotracheal tube of the lungs, and the hyoid bone, and Dr. Eckert responded that the endotracheal tube had been removed by Dr. Vachal, but his examination of the arteries and hyoid bone had revealed no damage.

"Now, were there any organs that had not been replaced in the child? In other words, that were not there at the time you had a chance to examine?" Quint continued.

"It seems to me that most all the organs were there so I could examine them at the time."

After the doctor had explained his findings regarding the internal organs, Quint asked for the doctor's opinion on the cause of death.

"Doctor, at the conclusion of your gross examination of this body was there anything that you could tell that gave the appearance of something other than normal death?"

"Other than natural death?"

"Other than a natural death."

"No," the doctor said firmly.

Quint had him rule out all typical signs of suffocation. Then he had him testify about his microscopic examination of the organ tissues. Eckert said he had found evidence of chronic inflammatory cells, viral cells, primarily in the child's liver and lungs, but the infection had extended to the child's larynx, esophagus, and intestinal tissue.

Quint wanted to know what had caused the child's death.

"Was a viral infection," Eckert said with a tone of finality. "It was the basic cause of the child's death."

A recess was taken before Pierce was allowed to cross-exam the doctor, but when the session reconvened, he stood up and walked toward the witness stand. He was excited, hyperactive, and his face was flushed. He paced back and forth with quick movements and asked his questions in a loud, aggressive voice.

"Now, Dr. Eckert, from a gross-examination point of view is it your testimony that all of the organs and organ systems of the deceased, José Lumbrera, were normal or within the normal range?"

"That I saw?"

"Yes."

"There was a larynx that was not seen, but I saw it microscopically."

Pierce wanted to know about Eckert's microscopic examination of *all* the tissue slides.

"Do you have a microscope at the place where you work?"

"Yes."

"And—"

"But, I looked at these at the hospital," Eckert interrupted, "St. Francis Hospital, where they have a much more powerful scope."

"And, in fact, isn't it true, Doctor, that at that hospital you consulted with other pathologists?"

Eckert had mentioned in his final autopsy report that he had consulted with other pathologists and that they had agreed with his findings.

"Sure. Certainly."

"And one of those pathologists that . . . you talked with and got his opinion was a resident by the name of Mr. Candela; is that correct?" (A resident physician is a physician who is employed by a hospital while receiving specialized training. In other words, he is still a student.)

"Well, I didn't consult with him. He was there . . . when I did it, but I consulted with Dr. John Richardson. He was a staff pathologist."

"And Dr. Richardson won't be here to testify today, will he?"

"No. He moved down to Texas."

". . . Colleagues," Pierce clarified, emphasizing the plural as he read from the doctor's report. "How many *colleagues* besides the doctor you testified to?"

"Well, the man I had particular reference to was Dr. Richardson. He had shown it to another colleague, and I can't recall the name. He was there at St. Francis," the doctor reluctantly admitted. Eckert began to fidget with his eyeglasses, positioning them, then repositioning them on the same spot on his nose.

"Now, at St. Francis they have an electron microscope, don't they, sir?"

"I don't know. I never use it."

"But isn't it true that an electron microscope can actually photograph or document the actual existence of the virus; isn't that correct?"

"I suppose. I have never used an electron microscope." The witness chair was on a swivel base, and the doctor began to move it slightly from side to side.

"These exhibits that have been marked as Defendant's C, D, E, F and G, are these photographs of the virus?"

"No. That's the pathological findings at different levels of review of the slides. In other words, low power, high power."

"Isn't it true with a regular microscope, Doctor, light microscope, you can't see virus?"

"You can see viruses," Eckert argued.

"You can?"

"Sure. You can see the viral bodies in certain of the larger viruses."

"Okay. In certain *larger* virus, but in these photographs—"

"Well," interrupted the doctor, "I wasn't looking for viruses. Of course, that's another area of expertise."

"You're not a virologist, are you, Doctor?"

"No, I'm not."

"Now, what is the name of the virus that killed José Lumbrera?" Pierce stopped in place and stared at the doctor.

"I have no idea," Eckert replied. "It was not identified."

"Now, you don't have any photographs of that virus to present to the jury today; is that correct?"

"I— yeah. I don't have any available, no, and neither does Dr. Vachal, because we didn't get anything from her."

Pierce wasn't going to let Eckert place any blame on Eva Vachal for the sloppy work he'd done. "Did you request anything from Dr. Vachal in regard to blood samples so that they could be tested in an electron microscope to determine the existence of viral—"

"They can't detect them in a viral electron microscope," Eckert interrupted.

"They can't detect with an electron microscope?"

"No, not blood. It has to be fixed and properly preserved."

"Did you cut any sections out yourself, Doctor, of the tissue when you did the second autopsy?"

"No."

"Now, these photographs that you've looked at and you've testified to, that you've identified, those photographs only deal with certain organs; isn't that correct, Doctor?"

"Yes. The organs— the organs that I selected were the liver and the lung, which I felt would provide the court with adequate information to back up my diagnosis."

"And you had no photographs of the heart, the brain, or the kidneys?"

"We didn't have time."

"Now, Doctor, you've indicated the heart was normal—"

"Well, I'm sorry," said the doctor, obviously not sorry at all. "I don't think I did. I didn't see anything in the heart that was grossly abnormal, but I did see and noted the fact that there were— there was the presence of a viral infection in the heart."

"Now, Doctor," Pierce said, moving closer and looking Eckert directly in the eye, "what if I were to tell you that after you've testified now, that the heart, the lungs, the larynx, the stomach, the esophagus, the duodenum, the appendix, and part of the diaphragm were *never, ever* sent to you, and you *never, ever* examined those?"

Eckert paused and repositioned the glasses on the bridge of his nose. He looked confused and flustered.

Pierce stared at the doctor and waited, but he could hear movement in the jury box. Out of the corner of his right eye he could see the last two jurors in the front row, and they had both leaned forward as they also waited for Eckert's reply.

"I don't know," he said finally. "I do know that I got microscopic sections of them and that's what I base my diagnosis on."

"But you've testified in direct examination you looked at the liver and you looked at the lungs. Isn't that correct?"

"I did, yeah," he admitted.

"Now, also, Doctor, you're basing your entire diagnosis on microscopic slides; is that correct?"

"My basic diagnosis of what?"

"Of natural death?"

"I'm basing it on everything I examined, including the child and the gross examination and the microscopics."

"But the gross examination showed no abnormalities; is that correct?"

"Sure. That's part of the— part of the examination," Eckert huffed, the color rising in his face.

Quint was shocked by Pierce's revelation that the doctor had never even seen those organs. He sat stone-faced and listened.

Pierce continued his questioning. He brought up the petechiae; the doctor didn't think it was important. He brought up the linear hemorrhage in the conjunctiva of the right eye; the doctor said it was probably due to dryness. He brought up the doctor's conclusion as to the child's cause of death; the doctor said the cause was a massive viral infection. Then he brought up the conversation Eckert had had with Detective Ken Elliott.

"Do you remember telling Detective Elliott that you felt the child died from natural causes and felt it was a gastrointestinal tract infection within the victim?"

"I think that was before I got the slides."

"Did you also tell Detective Elliott at that time and remind him that you were being employed by Michael Quint?"

"I don't know about employed. I was consulted by Mr. Quint."

"So, you don't remember whether you said it exactly that way?"

"I don't use the word employ."

"Basically a forensic pathologist has to be independent and maintain his neutrality; is that correct?" Pierce asked.

"Certainly. That's what I try to do," he replied defensively.

"Now, Doctor, let's go backwards here and see what you did in regard to the history of the deceased, José Lumbrera. Did you talk with Dr. Lauren Welch, the surgeon that was there administering to the child at the time of death?"

"I don't know. The only one I talked to, to save some time, is Dr. Vachal. She sent a listing of information in her epicrisis [evaluation], which is in her autopsy, which I felt was adequate, and also I was told that the child did die and was brought to the hospital. So, I had no records of the specific time that this happened."

"Did you request, Doctor, that more information such as the medical history and all the doctor's reports and all the investigative reports be sent to you prior to you making your final diagnosis?"

"No," Eckert reluctantly admitted. "Well, I think Mr. Quint had sent this—some of this material to me, but I don't—I don't—didn't require it to give an impression based on the autopsy."

Pierce wanted to know how much Eckert actually knew about the crime scene. "Doctor, what kind of surface was the child on when the child passed away?"

"In here— in Garden City?"

"Yes."

"I have no idea."

"You talked about you examined the nose for fibers. Is that correct?"

"Yes."

"Isn't it true that in the embalming process that many of those fibers and matters like that, natural fibers and so forth, would be removed during the embalming?"

"Unless it is looked at immediately you can't see those things."

"And you didn't look at it immediately; you looked at it after embalming."

"I looked at it days later after the kid was buried."

"Would a plastic sack or plastic bag, would that produce any fibers in the nostril areas?"

"Not that I know of unless it was a towel or something over the child."

"Now, let's go into your diagnosis and test it with the facts, Doctor."

"And test it what—"

"We're going to go over your diagnosis and look at how the condition of the child would be in your diagnosis. You indicate it's a chronic viral infection; is that correct?"

"Certainly!"

"And it would be over a considerable period of time."

"No."

"How much?"

"Well, it depends on the type of virus, but a virus and a death from a virus can be [of] a very rapid nature. I've had experience with my own kids."

"You testified on direct that there was *chronic* viral infection?"

"Right. But chronic, you have to— to understand what chronic means to a doctor now. A chronic infection could be a very rapid course or it could be a protracted course, maybe two or three months, you see. I don't know what— I can't recall exactly what I said the period of time would be."

Pierce then asked a series of questions designed to show the jury how little Dr. Eckert actually knew about the child's medical condition within the twenty-four-hour period leading up to his death. The doctor's replies showed that he had no idea how sick the child had been on the night of April 30 or on the night of May 1 when he died.

"Now, let's take this child at the time of death, the time that he expires. What caused that expiration? Is it an organ system that fails?" Pierce asked.

"Why did he die? Is that your question? Why did he die?" Perspiration was beginning to form on the doctor's upper lip.

"Yes."

"I think he was overwhelmed by the infection. That's called the viremia, which we haven't added to our armamentarium today."

Judge Nyswonger looked down at the doctor and said, "Your *what*?"

"That's a $10-term," the doctor replied with a smirk.

Pierce smiled at the doctor and nodded his head knowingly but kept focused on his objective. "Now, with somebody who had had a severe viral infection like you've talked about, would there be a fever?"

"I think— I'm sorry. You better repeat it. I didn't exactly get what you had mentioned."

"In this viral infection that you said just recently caused his death, this overwhelming viral infection, would there be a fever at the time that he passed away?"

"I can't say."

"Would he be bedridden at the time that he passed away, unable to get out of bed?"

"I would think so."

"What about two hours before his death, would he be able to get out of bed?"

"I have no idea. I can't really say. I don't know this case, this child's history well enough to be able to— and also would have had to know a little bit about the child in life."

"And so, that's one of the duties of a forensic pathologist is to get in and get all the facts and—"

"Your Honor, objection!" yelled Quint, jumping to his feet. "I think we are being argumentative at this point."

Judge Nyswonger agreed, so Pierce changed his question. He asked what had been the time of the child's death. Eckert didn't know. Pierce wanted to know if there had been any amoxicillin in the child's blood at the time of his death. The doctor couldn't remember.

Pierce glowered at the doctor for a moment, then turned and walked back to the counsel table. "Your

Honor," he said, "I have no further questions of this witness. Thank you."

When Pierce sat down, he clasped his hands and placed them on the table in front of him so that no one would notice how badly they were trembling. Then he sat quietly and listened while Quint tried unsuccessfully to shore up Eckert's flagging credibility.

Quint's last witness was the defendant, Diana Lumbrera, and as she took the stand, he prayed that she would show the jury the kind of grief that one would expect from the mother of a recently dead child. Much to his disappointment, Diana couldn't work up the enthusiasm.

"Diana, your name is what?"

"Diana Lumbrera," she said in a soft voice.

"You're going to have to talk a lot louder than that."

"Diana Lumbrera."

"And how old are you, Diana?"

"Thirty-one."

"How long have you lived in Garden City?"

"For five years."

"And what do you do, what's your profession?"

"I work for Monfort [in the] box department."

Quint asked her what tasks were involved in her job and how much she was paid. He asked her about her health insurance and about the life insurance policy she had taken out on herself and her son in April 1989.

"Now, . . . who is the beneficiary on your insurance?"

"My son, José."

"Did you ever do anything else with that insurance policy?"

"Yes. I tried to cancel it, but—"

"When did you do that?" interrupted Quint.

"It was somewhere in February this year."

"Why did you want it canceled?"

"I just didn't feel like I needed it or anything. I just didn't want to have it anymore."

"Okay. Now, how did you go about trying to cancel it?"

". . . I filled out a little card that people from that insurance gave . . . to me, and I just mailed it in to the company."

"And did you cancel the insurance then?"

"Yes, I did."

"Okay. Is it in effect now?"

"They answered me back and told me that I couldn't—"

Pierce objected to this statement as hearsay, so Quint rephrased his question.

"Is— was the insurance policy in effect on May 1st when your son died?"

"I think so. It was."

"Okay. And in looking at the policy, what does the policy say was the amount on your son?"

"To tell you the truth," she said very matter-of-factly, "I never did look at the policy."

"Did you know how much it was?"

"Until when [the funeral director] said it was $5,000, but otherwise I didn't even know how much it was."

"Okay. Thank you, Diana," Quint said, trying to appear confident as he strode back to his chair.

Pierce had only one question he wanted answered. "Now, Diana, you *knew* that there was a policy of insurance at the time of death that was in full force and effect covering little José's life; isn't that correct?"

Hatred for this man surged through Diana, but she managed to look confused. "Well, what do you mean?" she said innocently. "Explain to me better."

"Okay. When José died on May 1, the next day on May 2 you went to the funeral home and talked with [the funeral director]; isn't that correct?"

"Yes, I did."

"And did [she] at some time during those conversations on May the 2nd, 1990, indicate to you that the method of payment would be an important thing we need to consider for the funeral expenses and so forth?"

"No, I don't recall that."

Diana couldn't recall any of the things Pierce asked next, and he finally returned to his chair. Then the judge excused her from the witness stand.

Shirley turned and looked at the jury. She knew they were still having a very difficult time accepting a mother's guilt. She wondered what they had thought about Diana's testimony and her total lack of emotion.

Chapter 26

The trial entered the rebuttal phase on day five. Pierce called his two expert pathologists to negate the testimony given by the famous Dr. William G. Eckert. First came Dr. Michael Baden.

When Dr. Baden walked into the courtroom, Pierce turned to look at his witness and was more than a little surprised by what he saw. The back of the room had filled with medical personnel, and more medical workers had gathered in the hallway outside. These people had come to see Michael Baden. Some of them had even come to get his autograph.

Pierce hadn't know that Dr. Baden was such a big name in his own profession, but then he remembered that it was Dr. Vachal who had loaned him Baden's book. It was a book that was informative and entertaining for lay readers, but it was packed with important information and sound advice for people working in the medical and law enforcement fields. Baden's celebrity status among his peers suddenly made perfectly good sense.

Dr. Baden had a black mustache, heavy eyebrows, and black curly hair that had been tousled by the wind. He was dressed in an expensive dark suit and tie and carried a large traveling case at his side. He stepped up on the stand, adjusted his eyeglasses, and nodded his head. He was ready.

He was sworn in, then Pierce led him through a series of questions about his background, his introduction into the Lumbrera case, and the case materials he had used for his analysis. Baden's responses were personable, professional, and polished. He was very well prepared. He knew all the facts of José's medical history, the two autopsies, the circumstances surrounding his death and the scene of the crime.

Pierce finally asked him about his findings. "Do you have an opinion, Doctor, as to any sort of abnormality or any sort of, oh, life-threatening disease that's shown on those slides?"

"My opinion after reviewing the slides," Baden replied with a slight New York accent, "is that there was no evidence of natural disease that would have been a possible cause of death in the child, and the slides essentially were normal for a four-year-old." The doctor then explained what "normal" meant in relation to the organs of a human at various stages of growth.

"Doctor, did you see any evidence in any of these slides of any sort of life-threatening viral infection?"

"No." The doctor went on to explain what he had seen that had led him to that conclusion. He ended by saying, "In my opinion not only wasn't there . . .

evidence of a viral infection, but there were no specific organs that were damaged."

Pierce continued his questions, and Baden showed his mastery of the facts in the case by answering them all in great detail.

Then Pierce finally got to the bottom-line question. "And do you have an opinion as to the cause of death of this child based upon your years of experience, your training and based upon your analysis of all the medical information in this case that you've examined and the slides and so forth? Do you have an opinion as to the cause of death of José Lumbrera?"

"Yes."

"What is that opinion, sir?"

"My opinion is this child was smothered to death."

Pierce thanked the skilled pathologist, took his seat and watched while Mike Quint tried to create doubt about the validity of the doctor's findings. Baden's answers were clear and to the point. He didn't need to cloud the issues; he had facts to back up his conclusions. Finally, Quint decided to made the doctor look like a hired gun, a man who would say whatever was needed just for the money he would receive.

"Doctor, let me be indelicate for a minute. What kind of fees do you request for your appearances? What are your standard fees?"

"Well, the fee that I'm ... charging in this instance is $150 an hour ... but in private work for non-municipalities it would be more than that as a physician."

"How much more?"

"$200 an hour."

Baden had not taken this job just for the money, but Quint's ploy was still effective. The jurors took a better look at Baden's tailored suit and his fancy briefcase and exchanged glances. A hundred and fifty dollars an hour wasn't much money to people from New york City, but it was an enormous amount of money to the folks who lived here. They wondered how objective this expert had been in reaching his conclusions.

Pierce's second expert pathologist, Dr. Harry Wilson, took the stand immediately after lunch. Wilson was in his early forties, with receding dark hair and a full beard. He was dressed casually in corduroy pants and a pullover sweater.

Many of the jurors still looked skeptical, and the prosecutor hoped that Dr. Wilson's testimony would provide them with the reassurance they obviously needed.

"Would you please state your name for the record, sir?"

"Harry L. Wilson," said the doctor in a deep, low voice.

Pierce had the doctor list his education, training, and experience for the jury. Dr. Wilson was a pediatric pathologist, a medical doctor trained as a pathologist, who understands and analyzes diseases in children. He said he specialized in interpreting tissue sections and disease processes in infants and children. He was obviously a dedicated professional who was passionate about his work.

Pierce asked him about his microscopic findings, then the doctor went through the various organs, relating all his findings to what would be considered normal in the body of a young child.

"Now, Doctor," Pierce interjected, "in any of these organs that you've examined, did you find any evidence of life-threatening viral or bacterial infection that would cause the death of José Lumbrera?"

"No," he replied firmly, "I did not. . . ."

Pierce wanted to know if a virus would produce a toxic effect in the cells of the body. Dr. Eckert had testified that this would happen.

The doctor explained that when viruses attacked cells, certain cells might produce some toxic products from those cells, but he had a better way to explain what one would expect to find in the body of a child who had a viral infection.

"One of the most sensitive glands to look for," he said, speaking directly to the jury, "is . . . the thymus gland. The thymus gland is a gland that we all as human beings have. It's a gland that is present in the fetus, present in the newborn baby and gets bigger as the child grows. By the time we're adults, this is a gland that goes away, and most adults don't know about this gland. But it's a very important gland for kids.

"It's located right in the front part of the chest, right under the top part of the breastbone in the chest. The thymus gland is the gland that helps the body develop normal immunity, and certain types of cells come from the thymus gland. If a child has a serious infection, if a child has serious stress, if a child has serious toxic events occurring, that thymus gland very rapidly undergoes changes where it starts shrinking in size, and microscopically you see changes in the cell distribution in the thymus gland. The pattern looks different as a reflection of stress and toxic events."

"Okay, Doctor, did you have a chance to look at the thymus gland of José Lumbrera?"

"Yes. I was able to view the microscopic slides of that thymus, and I noted the report in the autopsy that this thymus was of normal weight. It was 20 grams, which is an appropriate size for a four-year-old child. And the microscopic slides of that child's thymus gland show absolutely no stress or toxic-type injury changes. No stress changes in that thymus," he said, shaking his head to add emphasis. "Normal-looking thymus."

Pierce had a few follow-up questions, then he asked the doctor if he was on any boards in the state of Colorado.

"I am an active member of the Child Death Review Committee for the state of Colorado. I helped start that committee, and I personally review each death of each child in Colorado, both in and out of the hospital. In '89 we had about 750 deaths, and I reviewed those deaths by looking at the death certificates, reviewing the autopsies and reviewing other pertinent records." The doctor had served on that board for two years.

"One of the functions of our committee," he continued, "is to try to see that when a child dies, a reasonable explanation has been made available as to why that child died, and that means that if a child dies outside of a hospital, we need to look at the work done by the coroner's office, and if a child dies inside of a hospital, we need to look at the work done by the hospital in terms of evaluating why that child died. The ultimate purpose, of course, is to try to understand why kids die [in order to] keep kids alive. . . ."

"Okay, Doctor, based upon your experience as a pathologist and as a pediatrician, and based upon your observations that you made of these microscopic slides and the organs on a gross nature, did you have an opinion as to whether this child died from a severe viral infection?"

"Yes, I have an opinion."

"And what is that opinion, sir?"

"My opinion is that this child died not of a natural disease process such as a viral infection. There is no evidence in any of the anatomical material that this child died of a viral infection."

"Have you in this specific case done an examination and an evaluation of what you feel would be the cause of death of José Lumbrera?"

"Yes, I have."

"And what have you looked at to try to ascertain the cause of death of this child?"

"What one looks at is what the autopsy findings were and what they weren't. This autopsy on this child is what's known as a negative autopsy. It's an autopsy that doesn't have an anatomical cause of death, and whenever a pathologist, forensic or hospital-based pathologist, finds a negative autopsy, you go through a list of things to eliminate that might have resulted in the death and a negative autopsy finding. . . ."

Pierce waited until the doctor finished, then he got to the gist of the matter.

"My opinion," said Wilson, "is that this child died suddenly and unexpectedly from non-natural means. There is no natural disease process evident in this child's body to account for why this child was dead. I think that the non-natural means had to be something that you relate to the historical circumstance, and therefore, it becomes very important to know what is the circumstance under which this child was found dead. The presence of the petechiae as they were found in the emergency room and at the autopsy strongly supports that this child died from an asphyxial event. How that asphyxiation occurred I don't know because I wasn't there, and that's where the circumstance becomes important. An accident could have occurred where someone did something to asphyxiate the child. That has to relate to the circumstance."

Pierce would have preferred a good "The child was smothered to death" reply, but he couldn't criticize this doctor for being thorough. After all, it was Dr. Eckert's failure to be thorough that had caused all the problems in the first place. He thanked Dr. Wilson, then returned to his chair.

Quint walked around in front of the witness

stand, smiled at the bearded man, and began asking questions aimed at impeaching him and his testimony. It didn't work. Finally he tried the "hired gun" tactic that had worked so well with Dr. Baden.

"Now, in your work at the Children's Hospital," Quint said, "are you working basically as a private physician? In other words, are you— how do I want to put this? Do you have a private practice?"

"No. I'm full-time employed on a straight salary by the Children's Hospital in Denver, and for my salary they expect me to do a certain number of autopsies, a certain number of surgical evaluations, and to run the hematopathology [blood analysis] laboratory; and I am also free then to pursue the various educational and death-review activities that I do, which I do on a volunteer basis."

Quint heard the words "on a volunteer basis" and thought better about asking the doctor if he had received any compensation for the time he had spent on this case. Had he asked that question, the answer would have been no. As always, Dr. Wilson had given freely of his time because he hoped his efforts would help save the lives of other children.

Quint could see that the jury liked Dr. Harry Wilson, and he had to find a way to change that. He took one more shot. He thought he might be able to make the doctor look like an activist with a hidden agenda.

"And these are on the child abuse boards you participate with and Dr. Beckman's group as well; those kinds of activities?"

"Yes, and I also provide my volunteer services to

the Indian Health Service and the Public Health Service to help them with reviewing infant and child deaths—"

Quint held up his palm to stop the doctor and said, "Very good, Doctor. . . ." Then he returned to his chair, regretting that his failed attempts to impeach the man had only made him look better.

A half-hour later both attorneys made their closing arguments. Pierce asked for a guilty verdict of first-degree murder. He argued that Diana had murdered her son not only for the insurance money his death would bring, but for relief from the $250 in expenses it cost her each month to support him.

Quint argued that reasonable doubt as to the real cause of the child's death still existed, so they had no choice but to come back with a not-guilty verdict. He reminded them about the conflicting evidence that had been put forth by equally qualified experts. And he appealed to their basic human instinct to believe that a mother would never murder her child for money.

Judge Nyswonger then gave the jurors their instructions and sent them into a room down the hall to deliberate. It was 3:45. They discussed the case for an hour, then recessed for the evening.

The next morning Pierce sat at the counsel table, leaning forward on his elbows and playing nervously with a ballpoint pen. He looked at his watch; it was nearly eleven o'clock.

Mary Ann Shirley's anxiety showed in the heel of

her right foot, which kept tapping rhythmically on the floor as the seconds ticked by.

Quint sat motionless, staring at some notes in front of him.

A group of anxious reporters and determined spectators waited in the seats at the back of the courtroom. Over a dozen members of Diana's large extended family had driven up the night before, and they also sat at the back, whispering among themselves as they waited impatiently for the jury to return. Pierce could feel their hostile stares on his back.

Suddenly the door behind the judge's bench swung open and Diana and a deputy sheriff walked in. Diana had slept poorly, and she hadn't bothered with makeup, so her face looked ashen with dark circles beneath her eyes. She looked up, saw her family, and smiled. She had just taken her seat when Judge Nyswonger walked into the room.

The bailiff asked everyone to stand as the judge climbed onto the bench and took his seat. A few seconds later the twelve regular jurors filed in one by one. They had deliberated for only three hours before reaching a unanimous verdict.

Diana crossed her arms in front of her chest and stared nervously up at the judge.

Judge Nyswonger looked over at the jury foreman and asked if the jury had reached a verdict.

"Yes, Your Honor, we have," answered one of the male jurors sitting in the front row.

"Would you please hand the form of the verdict to the bailiff, please? Miss Lumbrera, I'd like to ask if you'd stand, please? Members of the jury, I would ask that you listen as I read your verdict aloud."

Diana and Mike Quint stood up, and the judge read from the slip of paper he had been handed.

"We the jury, impaneled and sworn, do upon our oaths find the defendant guilty of murder in the first degree."

Pierce heard Diana gasp, then start to cry. He felt a wave of incredible relief and had to repress a sudden urge to jump up and scream with joy. He heard movement behind him and looked back. Diana's family was rushing up to comfort her.

If Pierce hadn't felt so good at that moment, he would have become furious. He wondered why her family had never offered that same kind of comfort and support to her helpless babies. Why they had always looked the other way as she cruelly murdered child after child? To him, Diana, was a monster who took sick pleasure in torturing little children, a monster who would take them to the brink of death, then let them live until she decided it was time for them to die. She was evil—frighteningly evil. He was very glad that she would pay for her heinous crimes by spending most of the rest of her life in prison. He prayed he would never have to see her again.

Chapter 27

Texas Ranger Warren Yeager and his wife, Phyllis, drove to Garden City, picked up Diana Lumbrera, and transported her back to Farwell, Texas. She was to stand trial on three counts of capital murder.

Parmer County was rural, sparsely populated, and very poor. There was not enough money in the county budget to pay for one capital murder trial, not to mention three. Adjacent Bailey County, which had charged Diana with one count of first-degree murder, also lacked sufficient funds to pay for a long, complicated murder trial. The county commissioners in both counties told their prosecutor, Johnny Actkinson, that they would impose a special tax on the county residents to raise funds for the trials—*if* he thought the trials were really necessary.

Actkinson took his time and considered everything. He looked at the fifteen-year sentence that Diana had received in Kansas, and the fact that it was still on appeal. He looked at Diana's upcoming trial in nearby Lubbock County, and the additional time he hoped she would spend in prison for that first-degree murder. He calculated the amount of money that would have to be raised through such a tax and the consequence of that tax on the county taxpayers. He weighed the chances of winning four murder convictions.

Several months went by, and he finally decided it would be better to plea-bargain with Diana then to take her to trial. He and Diana's attorney, Selden Hale of Amarillo, reached an agreement in early summer of 1991. Diana would plead nolo contendere to one count of first-degree murder, the murder of Melinda Ann Garza in 1982. In return, she would serve one life sentence only. All charges against her for the murders of Joanna, Melissa, Ericka, and even the Castro County murder of Christopher, would be dropped. Such a life sentence in Texas was equal to seven years or less before becoming eligible for parole.

Diana was then transported to Lubbock County to stand trial for the first-degree murder of her infant son, José Luís. Lubbock County was large, well-populated, and relatively wealthy; money to prosecute Diana was not a serious issue. But politics apparently were. District Attorney Travis Ware had always said that he used selective prosecution to keep the killers off the streets. In a 1994 reelection speech he put it this way: "The reason we have prioritized is because they are the most dangerous criminals out there." Apparently, a serial baby killer wasn't dangerous enough, *if* that killer killed only Hispanic babies.

Ware and his assistant, Rebecca Atchley, readily entered into a generous plea bargain with Diana through her Lubbock attorney, Tony Wright. In exchange for a plea of nolo contendere, Diana would receive one life sentence to be served *concurrently* with the one in Parmer County. That meant Diana would serve no additional time for the Lubbock murder of her infant son. And Ware and Atchley could write the case off as a conviction they had won.

Diana Lumbrera was clearly relieved when her Texas ordeal was over. She had a good reason to feel relieved; she would serve less than seven years in Texas for the brutal murders of six tiny children. She had still gotten away with murder.

After the Lubbock hearing was over, Diana was transported to the Kansas Correctional Institute for Women in Lansing, Kansas, where she began serving out her fifteen-year sentence. Eighteen months later that conviction was overturned by the Kansas State Supreme Court. The reason cited was "an accumulation of trial errors." The court felt that, among other things, Diana's trial should have been held in a different venue, and individuals with knowledge of Diana's other dead children should have been disqualified from serving on the jury.

Chapter 28

It was Monday, February 1, 1993, and Kansas was
suffering through the coldest winter it had experienced in over a decade. John Wheeler, newly
elected Finney County attorney, leaned forward in
the large leather chair, clasped his hands together
on the desk, and stared hopefully at Ricklin Pierce.
Wheeler had just asked Pierce to serve as prosecuting attorney for Diana Lumbrera's retrial in Great
Bend, a little town 125 miles northeast of Garden
City.

Pierce already knew that Diana's conviction had
been overturned. He had hoped Wheeler would
retry her for José's murder, but he had never
guessed for a moment that Wheeler would ask him
to serve as prosecutor in that retrial. He began to
get a very bad feeling in his gut as he thought about
Wheeler's request.

He was rested, his legal practice was slow,
Wheeler would give him all the assistance he
needed—secretarial help, the use of the telephones,

a police investigator, etc.—that was the up side. The down side was that it would be harder to win a conviction this time, because Quint would know all of his evidence and the strategy he would be using. Quint wouldn't be caught off guard a second time. Serving as prosecutor would require an enormous amount of effort, too many sleepless nights, and a lot of trips out of town. And just the fact that he'd have to see Diana again was reason enough to say no.

Pierce felt the intensity of Wheeler's stare and squirmed slightly in the chair. He didn't want to go through this again. He looked out the window, stalling for time, trying to find a decent way to say no. Nothing came to him.

"Rick, Texas was too easy on this woman," Wheeler said, "and with credit for time served, she'll be back on the street in about four years. We don't really have the money for a retrial, but I don't think we've got a choice here; once she's out, she'll probably kill again.

"Now you know I'd do this myself," Wheeler continued, "if I had enough time to prepare, but I don't. There's only eighty days left, and I don't even know the facts of this case. You're the only one who can do it, and if you say no. . . . Well, are you willing to have that on your conscience?"

Pierce sighed and slumped back in his chair. "Okay, where do we start?"

In Kansas, when a verdict is overturned by the state supreme court, the county attorney has only ninety days in which to begin retrying the case. That means the jury must be selected, sworn in, and evidence presented no later than the ninetieth day. If that time limit is exceeded, the prosecution of the defendant will automatically be terminated.

The ninety-day clock had started on Friday, January 15, 1993, right after Wheeler took office, so more than two weeks had already elapsed. In fact, the first pre-trial hearing in Great Bend had already been held, and it was there that John Wheeler had realized he wouldn't have sufficient time to prepare for such a complicated case.

When Pierce returned to his office, he put his other work on hold and made a comprehensive list of everything he thought would have to be done in preparation for the trial. Every prosecution witness from the first trial would have to be located and subpoenaed—and there was a new element that would require considerable time and effort.

Pierce wanted to introduce the Texas murders of José Luís and Melinda in the second trial, because Diana had pled nolo contendere to those murder charges as part of her Texas plea bargains. If the judge allowed that evidence, it would go a long way toward establishing Diana's killing pattern. Pierce knew a hearing would have to be held to determine the admissibility of those two murders, so he needed to learn about them as quickly as possible. That meant the Texas witnesses would have to be located and interviewed, and certified copies of all related documents obtained.

Pierce worked on the list for two days, and when it was complete it contained the names of fifty-one prosecution witnesses and more than four dozen documents. He was ready to work with an investigator. None of the former detectives was available to help him. James Hawkins had been promoted to captain and reassigned to the administrative division. Mike Utz had been promoted to sergeant and put in charge of the office of professional standards. Ken Elliott had returned to Colorado and was working as a deputy for Sheriff Richard Shockley in the Larimer County Sheriff's Department. So Detective Robert Goeman had been assigned to help.

Goeman was a tall, lanky man in his late forties with blond hair, a deep voice, and a habit of smoking long, thin cigars. Goeman had been a tunnel rat in Vietnam, which meant his job had been to crawl through dark underground tunnels to search out Vietcong. The job had required an unusual amount of determination, and over the years he had retained that quality.

Pierce walked down to the LEC and gave Goeman a copy of the list he had made. Goeman set to work immediately. Like Pierce, he knew how important it was to keep Diana in prison and how little time was left to get everything done.

There were problems from the start. Many of the witnesses had moved—some out of state, some even out of the country, and some of the original Texas documents were missing. Then Quint hired two additional experts: Dr. Charles Reiner, a pediatric pathologist from Ohio, and Dr. Michael Hughson, an associate professor of pathology at the University of Oklahoma Health Sciences Center in Oklahoma

City. Pierce was concerned that these men might be hired guns who would agree with Dr. Eckert's findings. Three expert defense pathologists declaring the death to be from natural causes would certainly confuse the issues, especially since the famous Dr. Eckert wouldn't be making the same blunder about the missing organs this time.

A few weeks had passed when Pierce learned of the new experts' conclusions: Hughson agreed with Dr. Eckert that the child had died from a viral infection; Reiner said he had also found a viral infection throughout the child's body, but he thought there might be several possible causes for the boy's death; one of those was suffocation. Overall, the news was bad enough to justify Pierce's concern.

The trial date was nearing when Pierce finally received his first bit of good news. Judge Barry Bennington ruled that the two Texas deaths would be admissible for the purposes of showing Diana's intent (premeditation) and motive. Pierce's confidence returned; the only thing standing between him and a guilty verdict was the testimony of the two new experts. He pushed everything else aside and concentrated on preparing to cross-examine them.

Chapter 29

An elderly man in a faded gray suit was first in line outside the locked doors of Judge Bennington's district courtroom. Behind him were some familiar faces, others who also came regularly to see the real-life dramas of people on trial. At half-past eight a deputy came and unlocked the doors, then the crowd flooded in and filled up the seats.

The room was small and warm and felt very old— maybe it was the faded oak paneling or the old-fashioned trim or the slightly musty smell of the curtains. Space was so limited that the two counsel tables had been pushed together in an L shape in the area in front of the judge's bench.

Pierce walked in and took his assigned seat; it was on the long side of the L facing the jury box. Diana and Quint were already sitting perpendicular to him at their table to his right. He would have preferred any other configuration possible except this one.

Diana's large extended family had driven up from

Texas and New Mexico to attend the entire trial. They were now seated in the first three rows on the right side of the visitors' gallery and were waiting nervously for the trial to begin. Their presence seemed to add an ominous quality. Pierce wouldn't allow himself to look at them, but he couldn't avoid feeling their hostility.

At exactly nine o'clock, Judge Barry Bennington walked in and took his seat on the bench. Judge Bennington was a likeable man, thin with receding brown hair, a dry sense of humor, and a predisposition to act cautiously. He had no intention of making any errors that would provide grounds for yet another retrial. A minute later the jury filed in, then the judge called the trial into session.

This jury was similar to the first one. It was evenly divided as to gender, all were Caucasian except for one Hispanic grandmother, and most were middle-aged. But none of them had ever heard of Diana Lumbrera.

As the judge instructed them on their responsibilities, Pierce thought about the strategy he would use in this trial. He knew it would be a long trial because the combined witness list totaled more than seventy-five witnesses, and some of them would probably be recalled to testify a second time. That meant he would have to sell the jury on his case as early as possible. If he tried to feed them the facts piecemeal, they would get tired of trying to figure it out for themselves and become angry at him.

Pierce looked over at Diana and was surprised to see that she looked a lot older than she had at the first trial. There she had looked young and attractive, although cold and hardened, he thought. But now she looked middle-aged, closer to fifty years old than her actual thirty-four. She was also heavier, and her hair was cut shorter and had a dull, frizzy, overpermed look. But it was more than that. She seemed to have no fight left in her. She didn't look bored; she just looked tired. And she no longer looked evil; she just looked—*pathetic*. He saw her as the dried-up shell of a person who had lived a life filled with hatred, lust, and greed.

Pierce was partially right about Diana. She had changed. Spending nearly three years in jails and prison had worn her down and shattered her cockiness. Her hatred was still there, but it was hidden beneath her fear of spending another twelve years in a Kansas prison. This time she was willing to do whatever it took to look innocent, and appearing pitiful and broken was just part of her act. She would cry often, using the tissues that Quint provided for her.

Suddenly Pierce heard his name spoken; the judge had said he could make his opening statement. He quickly stood up, thanked the judge, then gave very brief opening remarks. He told the jury he was going to prove that Diana Lumbrera had murdered her four-year-old son the same way she had murdered two other children in Texas—by smothering them and for the purpose obtaining their life insurance monies and reducing her monthly expenses. He said he knew that such an act would seem incredible, even unthinkable, to the jury, because that's the way it appeared to every normal human being. And it was that very fact that had allowed Diana's crimes to go undetected for such a long time. But she *had* murdered her young son, and he would prove it to them.

Quint gave his opening statement next, then Pierce began presenting his case.

Over the next two days Pierce called his witnesses—the detectives, the medical people, Diana's coworkers, the people from her credit union, her landlord, the child's godmother—others. Each added his or her own piece of information to the dark and ugly picture that was forming—a picture of a mother who had murdered for money.

At the end of each day Pierce returned to his motel, ate alone in the dining room, then studied his notes before going to bed. His cases was unfolding just as expected, and just as expected the jury was having a very hard time believing that Diana had really murdered her little boy. They had even heard from Dr. Eva Vachal and Dr. Michael Baden and were still far from being convinced.

The next morning Pierce was walking down the hallway toward the courtroom when it happened for the third time; one of Diana's young family members rushed up in front of him and took his photo with a Polaroid camera. The girl was probably twenty years old and very pretty, but her eyes were filled with a terrible hatred. She seemed to be trying to intimidate him—perhaps letting him know that something very bad would happen to him if he didn't stop the prosecution of her sister.

Pierce ignored her and walked on by. He had more important things to think about; today he would begin calling his Texas witnesses to talk about the other two deaths. When the trial resumed, he began with the death of two-year-old Melinda.

Diana's former employer remembered how healthy Melinda had seemed the afternoon before her death and how strangely unaffected Diana had been only hours following her funeral. The retired insurance agent talked about selling Diana a life insurance policy on the child and how Diana had called him at home early the next morning to say that Melinda had died. She wanted him to send her the insurance money. Other witnesses came and testified, their stories adding more details to the gruesome picture Pierce was painting.

Finally Pierce introduced a certified copy of the Texas Judgment of Conviction, the Parmer County plea-bargain document that Diana had signed—all references to the other four deaths had already been removed. He wanted the jury to know that she hadn't contested the murder charge.

The jurors turned and stared questioningly at her as she shook her head in denial and sobbed into a tissue.

The next day Pierce continued with the Texas people, this time bringing up those who had evidence regarding the 1978 murder of two-month-old

José Luís. He first called Tony Garza, Diana's first husband; then came the nurse from Methodist Hospital who had been on duty when Diana murdered the child. Last came Texas Ranger Warren Yeager to testify about Diana's conviction for first-degree murder.

As the evidence piled up, the jurors became increasingly uncomfortable with what they were hearing. They couldn't reconcile their impression of Diana with the terrible things they were hearing that she had done. It just didn't seem possible.

Pierce saved his two pathology experts until Friday afternoon, because he intended on having them tie all the pieces together. Bux would sum up his findings on the two Texas deaths, then Wilson would summarize the bigger picture of the three combined deaths in Texas and Kansas. That would give the jurors the whole picture to think about over the weekend. Pierce first called Dr. Robert Bux.

Bux was a handsome man in his early forties with dark hair and glasses. Pierce hoped the conservative jury would find this conservative Texan someone with whom they could identify and whom they could trust. Pierce had Bux describe his training and education, tell how he had been brought into the case to examine the deaths of José Luís and Melinda, and list those materials he had used in reaching his conclusions. He then focused on the doctor's findings.

He gave the doctor two hypothetical situations, which were actually the facts of the circumstances surrounding the deaths of José Luís and Melinda.

Then he asked the doctor for his opinion based on those two hypothetical situations, plus all the other materials he had reviewed.

"Would that be able to give you enough information with what you've already testified to to make a diagnosis in regard to Melinda Ann Garza?" Pierce asked.

"Yes, sir."

"And what would that be, sir?"

"That she died as a result of an asphyxial death, and it's a homicide," the doctor said confidently.

"And how would you term that . . . of José Luís?"

"I'd term it by itself as at a minimum suspicious and most likely a homicide. Coupled with the second death it's undoubtedly a homicide."

Quint spent the next two hours trying his best to destroy the doctor's credibility and conclusions. However, Bux was a fighter and wouldn't cave in. The air became so electrified that when Quint was finished, everyone watched in silence as he walked back around the counsel table, jerked out his chair, and sat down—his face still red with emotion.

Pierce then called his last expert witness to the stand. The man was Dr. Harry L. Wilson. After qualifying the doctor, Pierce quickly zeroed in on the three deaths. He started with that of José Antonio Lumbrera.

Dr. Wilson said the child had died an unnatural death as a result of asphyxiation—probably suffocation.

"Were you also called upon to look at the death

of Melinda Ann Garza and José Luís Garza by law enforcement officials?"

"Actually, Dr. Vachal had asked me, and she and I together, after reviewing this death, participated in reviewing information from other deaths, and those are two children whose other deaths were reviewed."

Pierce asked the doctor what he had used in determining the cause of José Luís Garza's death. After the doctor's reply, Pierce asked him what he had concluded.

"That this is an unexpected death that is not adequately explained [by the autopsy findings]."

Pierce then asked about the death of Melinda. The doctor said her death was also unexpected and possibly unexplained.

". . . Now Doctor, if you were to take these three deaths together . . . would you be able to come to a diagnosis as to the death of the first two, Melinda Ann Garza and José Luís Garza?"

"Melinda Ann Garza, in my mind, is an unexpected and possibly unexplained death by itself. José Garza is an unexplained and unexpected death."

"By itself?"

"By itself. José [Antonio] Lumbrera is a death from asphyxiation, probably suffocation," he gently explained. "Now having that last death be a death by asphyxiation, it opens up the concept that the other two unexplained and unexpected deaths are probably also deaths by asphyxiation. So, in my mind, the last death makes the other two deaths suspect, and what one is dealing with are multiple deaths in which you don't have a good explanation for why that child is dead. And when you also then find out that the other two deaths occurred in the presence of the same caretaker, you're left with the conclusion that that caretaker intervened in some way to bring about those unexpected and unexplained deaths."

Pierce nodded his head in silent agreement and returned to his seat.

Quint's cross-examination lasted for nearly an hour, but like Bux, Wilson stayed firm about his conclusions. Afterward Pierce rested his case, and the judge adjourned the trial for the weekend.

Chapter 30

Monday came and went as Quint began the presentation of his case. He brought up witness after witness, each testifying in some way to Diana's innocence. Included were her family members, who took the stand and testified that Diana had always been a good and loving mother to her children.

Tuesday was the day of Quint's experts, a day that could make or break the case. The punctual judge called the trial into session at precisely nine o'clock, then Quint stood up and called the famous Dr. William G. Eckert to the stand.

Quint took the doctor through the same series of questions he had asked at the first trial, and the doctor answered each with confidence. When it came to the child's organs, Eckert made sure he had it right this time.

"Well, of course," he explained, "in this case the organs were saved in a plastic bag by the pathologist, and also by the folks in the funeral home who prepared the body. And so we . . .

looked for injuries in ribs, broken bones, something of that nature. . . ."

Pierce could feel his excitement start to build as adrenaline pumped into his bloodstream. Eckert wouldn't look at him. He kept his eyes focused on Quint or on the people in the jury box, who were fascinated by what he was saying.

Eckert continued, explaining away the suspicious signs the other doctors had mistakenly thought were signs of suffocation. Finally, Quint asked about the doctor's conclusions as to the real cause of the child's death.

". . . my opinion primarily was that there's no—no evidence of anything but natural death."

"No evidence of *what*?" Quint wanted the jurors to hear it again.

"Unnatural disease, nothing but a natural disaster— uh, natural disease death," the doctor corrected himself.

Pierce choked back a nervous laugh. He felt the doctor was right the first time: this case had been a natural disaster for him.

Quint gave the doctor another chance to make his findings clear. This time the doctor's voice was firm and confident as he answered.

"I said this confirms my opinion, that this . . . was a natural death without any evidence of a smothering." Then he added, "This is based on *thirty-five years* experience in this field."

When Pierce got up to cross-examine the doctor, the doctor looked at him and squirmed slightly in his chair. His forehead began to shine with perspiration.

Pierce wasted no time in beginning his attack. He fired question after question, demanding to know the name of the virus, why the doctor had changed his specific diagnosis from a gastrointestinal virus to a diffuse viral infection, why he had failed to make a virology test from blood that had been drawn from the victim, et cetera. Eckert returned the fire each time. The jurors were soon on the edge of their seats again; they were witnessing yet another bloody courtroom battle.

Finally Pierce challenged Eckert on the "organ blunder" he had made at Diana's preliminary hearing in June 1990. He handed Eckert a copy of the prelim transcript, pointed out the inconsistency in one of his statements, and told Eckert to read the answer he had given at the time. That portion of the transcript covered Eckert's statements about how he had examined the child's heart.

"Sir," Pierce directed, "would you look at page 166, the bottom of the page, line 24?"

"Okay."

"First of all, the question on line 22 was: 'Very good, you were just beginning to tell us about your findings *visually* on the heart.' And what's your answer, sir?"

"Well, I read the autopsy of this lady," Eckert began.

"No! What is your answer?" Pierce demanded.

". . . I say, said the heart appeared normal size by her autopsy."

"You *didn't say that!*"

"No, but I'm just saying—"

"Read for us!" Pierce ordered.

After a great deal of fencing, the pathologist reluctantly compiled. "The heart appeared of normal size grossly," he said in a voice not much louder than a whisper.

"No! Read a little louder so we can hear you."

"The heart appeared of normal size talking grossly, which is the external examination."

Pierce stared menacingly at the doctor. ". . . How could you have weighed that heart if you never saw it?"

"No, I didn't."

"Okay."

"But I'm— I'm referring to *her* autopsy."

Pierce gave the doctor a cynical look, shook his head, and said, "Let's go on to the—"

"No," Eckert said innocently, "I'm telling you the *truth!*"

Pierce had no mercy as he continued to hack away at Eckert's credibility. At the end everyone was tired, especially the aging doctor. However, he made one final attempt to justify his findings. He said José Antonio was very small and weak for his age, and those two factors were important considerations in his decision that the child had died from a viral infection.

"It's been testified that he was in the eighty percentile in regard to height for kids of his age," Pierce pointed out.

"But his size and his height were very small."

"So he could have easily been smothered by somebody who was stronger than he was, isn't that right?"

Eckert was tired, very tired. He shrugged his shoulders and said flatly, "Anything is possible."

It was late in the afternoon when Quint called his second expert witness, Dr. Charles B. Reiner. Reiner was in his late sixties, short and thin, with a full head of white hair. He had held a professorship at two colleges of medicine, where he had worked as a pediatric pathologist. He was now retired and working as a consultant in cases such as this one. Quint went over the doctor's professional training and experience, which were considerable, then focused in on his findings.

". . . And did you have an opportunity to review the autopsy reports of Dr. Vachal and Dr. Eckert?"

"Yes."

"And did you also have an opportunity to view slides that were taken by Dr. Vachal?"

"Yes."

"In reviewing this particular situation were you able to come up with any *alternates,* as depicted in your report, as to the reason why this child may have died?"

The doctor explained that he had found evidence of a systemic infection, a widespread infection throughout the child's body involving many of the organs, including the heart, lungs, liver, kidney, etc. However, he thought the infection wasn't strong enough to have caused the child's death.

Pierce felt a sudden wave of relief. Well, that just blew Eckert the rest of the way out of the ballpark, he thought.

"There are other possibilities," Reiner continued, "that would require other information that we don't have." He explained that one such possibility would be a hereditary metabolic disorder, which under certain circumstances could lead to a person's death. Yet another would involve the mechanical failure of the contraction of the heart. The doctor gave long, detailed explanations of what would be involved in these two conditions.

Pierce had spoken to Dr. Vachal about the doctor's findings, so he knew something about those two other possibilities, but not enough. It was the one area he hadn't had time to research thoroughly, and that fact was worrying him a great deal. He was still listening to Reiner when his attention was drawn to Mike Quint. Quint had reached below the table and brought out a slide projector.

Dr. Reiner had made photographic slides of cells from the tissues of the child's various organs. He wanted to show the jury exactly what condition those organs had been in. Quint set up the projector and dimmed the lights, then the doctor went through his prepared slide show. Each slide showed the infection in each organ—the heart, the bronchial tube (the airway that conducts air from the windpipe out into the lungs), the lungs, the water on the lungs. He listed the symptoms that would have been expected—respiratory distress, difficulty breathing, fast breathing, coughing, and expectory wheezing like an asthmatic.

Pierce sat up and frowned; José had shown none of those symptoms before this death. He was beginning to feel impatient. He wondered why this man was going on and on in such minute detail when he had already said that the child had not died from an infection? What was he trying to prove? Pierce had to force himself to relax. He glanced at his watch and saw that it was only four o'clock, which meant he would probably have to cross-examine the doctor today. There would be no chance to do additional research.

Suddenly Diana stood up and staggered toward the door behind the judge's bench. The shocked jurors watched as she stumbled, then fainted into the deputy's sheriff's arms. Several of her family members jumped to their feet but thought better of interfering with the deputy as he helped her out of the room. Reluctantly, they sat back down.

The judge interrupted Dr. Reiner and said to Quint, "Mr. Quint, your client has left the room. Do you wish to continue without her or do you wish to take a recess?"

Quint wasn't aware of Diana's apparent collapse, because his attention had been focused totally on the images on the screen. Much to Pierce's disappointment, Quint said, "I think it would be best if we just continue, Your Honor."

"Very well," said the judge. "You have no objection to continuing in her absence?"

"No, Your Honor," Quint said.

Dr. Reiner finished his slide show. Then Quint turned the lights up and asked, "Doctor, is it fair to say that in your evaluation there are open doors still left unresolved, in other words, there are potential reasons that this child died from a hundred percent anatomical natural death other than smothering?"

"Yes," he replied with confidence.

"I have nothing else, thank you, Doctor."

Pierce rose nervously to his feet, walked toward the witness stand and was thinking about what question to ask when the judge interrupted him. He said he was going to adjourn the trial until the following morning because of Diana's unexpected *illness*. Then the sound of a siren could be heard as an ambulance pulled into the courthouse parking lot. Outside, three attendants jumped out carrying a metal stretcher, rushed into the building, and returned carrying Diana Lumbrera. They put her in the ambulance and rushed her to a nearby hospital.

Pierce spent that evening finishing his research on Dr. Reiner's two alternative possibilities. When he finally went to bed, he reflected on the irony of Diana's dramatic scene in the courtroom. It was her own bid for sympathy that had given him the extra time he desperately needed.

Chapter 31

Pierce glanced down at his watch and knew that Judge Bennington would walk through the door in exactly two more minutes. He flipped through the papers in front of him to make sure they were all there. Yes, he was ready. He looked at Quint; he looked calm and confident. He looked at Diana; she was tired and ragged from fear, and her anger was beginning to show through. She looked even older than she had when the trial started. Then he made the mistake of looking back at her family and came eye to eye with one of her relatives. The woman stared at him with such hatred that it sent a momentary chill down his back. He quickly looked away, then the judge walked in and called the trial back into session.

Pierce had to eliminate both alternative causes of death that Reiner had listed in his report in order to be left with only the third possibility—smothering. He wasn't surprised that Quint had failed to mention smothering as one possibility when questioning the doctor the day before.

Pierce started with the obvious. He wanted to remind the jurors that José Antonio had *not* died from an infection. He picked up his copy of the doctor's report and went through the list of organs, asking the doctor about the degree of infection in each. The doctor admitted that the degree of infection in each was mild.

Pierce then challenged the possibility of a hereditary metabolic defect having been the cause of death. The doctor said he had pretty much ruled that one out because of the glucose level contained in the child's body.

The prosecutor then focused on a mechanical malfunction of the heart as a cause. The doctor agreed that a disease that might have led to such a malfunction, like myocarditis, would have probably left the heart muscle flabby. Earlier testimony showed that the heart muscle was perfectly normal.

Pierce finally asked the doctor about his experience with smothering deaths. "Now, Doctor, did you write any articles, of the many that are in your curriculum vitae, did you write any articles about smothering or children being smothered by their parents?"

"No."

"How many smothering cases have you dealt with in your career as a pathologist?"

"Well," Reiner admitted, "in our county the smothering cases go to the county coroner. So that I would deal with them only indirectly, not as a pathologist, but as a member of the Franklin County child fatality review team. . . . I could not say how many we've seen."

Pierce took one final but extremely important shot. He asked the doctor if he had considered the sudden, unexpected deaths of Diana's other two children in Texas in reaching his conclusions about this child's death.

The doctor said no. He had been given *some* material about their deaths, but he had not received the microscopic slides from their autopsies, so he had refused to consider them in reaching his conclusions about this case.

Pierce looked at the doctor and shook his head reproachfully. He hoped the jury was connecting up the dots and reaching the same conclusions he had reached—that Dr. Reiner was a very thorough scientist, but he had failed to consider the most important fact of all—the fact that José's death was part of a pattern of *multiple deaths*. He thanked the doctor and returned to his chair.

Quint's final witness was Dr. Michael Hughson. Hughson was a thin, middle-aged man with a deep voice and a habit of talking very slowly. Quint thought he would be his best expert witness, because his work included a considerable amount of research. Juries were generally impressed by research scientists.

Dr. Hughson said he had read Dr. Vachal's autopsy report and reviewed the tissue slides.

"In reviewing the slides," Quint asked, "what did you find as prominent in [them]?"

"Well, two things that were particularly prominent. One was a very severe inflammation of the heart. . . ." Hughson described how that inflammation had led to the death of muscle fibers in the child's heart.

"And then the second thing that was even more— even more conspicuous than the inflammation of the heart," the doctor continued, "was a really striking hepatitis . . ." He said that meant an infection in the liver. But he had also found an inflammatory process in the kidneys, pancreas, adrenal glands, esophagus, larynx, trachea, thymus, and lungs. He finished his answer by saying, ". . . And I might say inflammation in the heart in a forensic setting is one of the things that you look for as a cause of sudden, unexpected death."

". . . In your evaluation, were you able to reach a feeling as to what kind of infection— what kind was it, viral or bacterial, that we were looking at in these particular slides?"

"The involvement of the heart and liver," replied Hughson with authority, "is quite characteristic of what we associate with enterovirus infections in myocarditis in current practice and in the American community is associated with coxsackie virus infections."

"So what you were seeing was very characteristic of what you would entitle—"

"Coxsackie virus," Hughson said with finality.

Quint asked the doctor if he had used any medical reference books in reaching his conclusion, and Hughson said he had used a current textbook of virology and a medical journal article from a text-book in pediatric pathology.

"Doctor, when it comes down to the brass tacks or when it comes down to the end result, what kind of a diagnosis did you make as it relates to this child?"

"This— this child had a quite severe systemic infectious disease that I attribute to an enterovirus coxsackie virus, and the pathology I found was sufficient to be considered the cause of death and therefore be considered a death by natural causes."

The doctor then gave a lengthy, morbid-sounding, technical description of that infection and the terrible damage it had done to the child's body.

Pierce's mouth dropped open as he listened to the doctor's words. He knew that Dr. Eva Vachal, her pathology colleague at the hospital Dr. Bruce Melin, Dr. Michael Baden, Dr. Harry Wilson, and even Quint's own expert, Dr. Charles Reiner, had all reached the same conclusion about the viral infection in the child's body at the time of death—it had been minor, only a simple cold. It certainly wasn't strong enough to have killed him.

Pierce shook his head in wonder. Each one of Quint's three experts had testified that the child had had a viral infection, two saying the infection had killed him—only they couldn't agree on exactly what that virus was or exactly how it had brought about his death. The third expert was saying the infection was actually mild, then giving a set of different possibilities. If this was confusing to him, the jury would have to be baffled. His gut began to knot up as he thought about the "reasonable doubt" this had to be creating in the jurors' minds.

Quint was just finishing his direct examination. "So in summary of your diagnosis, did this child die of natural causes?"

"The pathology I found was sufficient to indicate that this child died of myocarditis [inflammation of the heart] and that the death was by natural causes."

". . . thank you, Doctor. I have nothing else."

Pierce stood up, walked around the table to the witness stand, and looked at the slow-talking expert. It angered him that this man was talking with such authority about matters that were outside his field of specialization. He wasn't a virologist. He was a general pathologist, just like Dr. Eva Vachal.

Pierce asked him if he had consulted with either Dr. Eckert or Dr. Reiner in reaching his conclusions. The doctor said he had not.

"Would it surprise you to learn, Doctor, that both Dr. Eckert and Dr. Reiner, both defense experts, have already testified that they did not believe that there was a life-threatening myocarditis in regard to this child?"

Quint jumped up and practically screamed his objection. The judge agreed, so Pierce tried it again in another form.

"Sir, would you have any explanation as to why Dr. Reiner would indicate that there was no myocarditis, or if there was, it was mild and not life-threatening after his examination of the same slides?"

"Well— any— any myocarditis is life-threatening," Hughson said defensively. "You know, the mildness or the severity of it really doesn't—in my view doesn't have much cogency as to whether it's a life-threatening process or not. I mean, we see sudden deaths with very, very slight involvement of the heart." A tiny line of perspiration was beginning to form on the slow-talker's forehead.

"And as for Dr. Eckert," Pierce continued, "if he indicated on cross-examination yesterday that specifically the cause of death was *not* myocarditis. Would you have any explanation for that?"

Quint jumped up and objected again, but the judge wanted to hear this man's answer. He overruled the objection and told the witness to answer the question if he had an opinion.

Hughson stared blankly at the prosecutor and said nothing, so Pierce finally asked, "Do you even know Dr. Eckert?"

"No, I do not," he said nervously.

"Then, I'll withdraw the question." Pierce walked silently to the other side of the courtroom, then turned and said, "Now, Doctor, isn't it true that a person can have myocarditis and still survive?"

"That's— that's correct."

Hughson had already testified that he had used only Dr. Vachal's autopsy report and the tissue slides she had prepared for his analysis. Pierce wanted the jury to know that Hughson hadn't bothered to examine the heart itself.

"Now, Doctor, did you know of the existence of the gross organs, that is, in particular the heart, were located at St. Catherine's Hospital in the custody of Dr. Vachal?"

"I— I wasn't sure whether the organs existed any longer or not," he stumbled. "I— I knew that there had been two autopsies performed, and I just— I didn't know what the— I didn't know where the organs were." Then he added defensively, "And my agreement with Mr. Quint was to review the slides and to issue a report based upon the examination of the slides."

"But it would be important, would it not, to look at the gross organs, especially the heart, when you're giving a diagnosis of myocarditis?"

"No, it would not. In fact, this is an area of some controversy in— in why myocarditis will kill some people and not others," he said, trying to sound scientific. Then he gave a long, confusing explanation of why such an examination wouldn't have helped in determining the cause of death.

When the doctor finished, Pierce shook his head and smiled. Dr. Eckert had already tried that trick, and it hadn't worked any better for him. Pierce stayed focused.

"So you didn't examine the gross organs, and you didn't make any request to examine [them]?"

"No. I did not."

Pierce had prepared well for this moment. He had researched the coxsackie virus and knew all of the symptoms one would expect to find in a person who had contracted it. The dead child had not displayed those symptoms. This was a virus the doctor had found in a textbook, and it sounded right, if one didn't know all the facts. And the doctor hadn't bothered to get all the facts.

Pierce took the doctor through each symptom, showing how it didn't match the child's condition, and ultimately proving that his diagnosis was wrong. At the end the doctor stepped quickly from the witness stand and hurried out the door. It wasn't easy being an expert proved wrong.

The rebuttal phase began the following day, and both attorneys called up witnesses they hoped would sway the jury to their side. Afterward, the closing arguments were given, then the judge gave the jury their instructions and sent them out to deliberate. It was Wednesday, April 22.

Chapter 32

Pierce stood in the corridor outside the courtroom, leaning against the wall and trying not to be impatient. It was nearly four o'clock on Thursday afternoon, and the jury had been deliberating for more then eight hours. He knew that was a very bad sign; with every hour that passed, his chances of winning a conviction were reduced. He was trying to focus his mind on something else when the bailiff suddenly opened the door and announced that the jury was coming back in.

Soon the courtroom had refilled with Diana's family, reporters, and the curious. Pierce, Diana, and Quint were in their seats at the counsel tables. When everyone was quiet, the judge walked in, followed by the jury, and called the trial back into session. Mike Quint stood up, then Diana reluctantly did the same.

"The bailiff has informed me that the jury has reached a verdict," Judge Bennington said, "and I see that Mr. Carson is carrying some papers. Does that mean you are the foreman?"

A tall man in the back row stood up and said, "Yes, sir, Your Honor."

"Has the jury reached a verdict?"

"Yes, we have, Your Honor."

"Will you deliver it to the bailiff? Just give it to the bailiff. Thank you." The tall man reached awkwardly over the head of a middle-aged woman in front of him and handed the papers to the female clerk.

"Will the clerk please read the verdict?" the judge said.

The clerk turned toward Judge Bennington and read, "In the District Court of Barton County, Kansas, Case Number 93-CR-15, State of Kansas versus Diana Lumbrera. Verdict. We, the jury, find the defendant guilty of murder in the first degree."

Diana cried out in a guttural, animal sound, then collapsed into her chair and began to genuinely sob.

It's early April 1994, and inside a dormitory of the Kansas Correctional Facility at Lansing, Kansas, Diana Lumbrera sits alone on the twin bed in her small room. Tacked on her walls are photos of her family, including some of her children, which were taken in the months before their deaths. Her sisters sent them to her. They were sure she'd find comfort in looking at all the people who loved her.

By her bed is a small chest filled neatly with her things, the only place of privacy she has left. She's dressed in blue jeans, a blue work shirt, and white tennis shoes, much the same kind of clothing she wore on the outside. On her shirt is stenciled the number 53601, her new identity in this small coed facility. Her file in the warden's office shows a projected release date of 2005, then transfer to a Texas prison for seven more years.

Diana looks remarkably better than she did a year ago at her trial. She's lost weight, grown her hair long, and started using makeup. She's attractive once again. When she goes outside, the two hundred male prisoners housed on the other side of the tall fence whistle at her and make catcalls. Is it possible that she still loves that kind of attention and still despises the men who give it to her?

Diana works hard at being a model prisoner, constantly finding ways to endear herself to the prison staff. There's a point system here, and as soon as she gets her points low enough, she'll be able to transfer to the minimum security unit. As a minimum security prisoner, she'll be eligible to join the prison's work furlough program, and that program will allow her to get work on the outside. That's probably what she thinks of most—being on the outside again. Those who put her here wonder what will happen then.